"As an Assistant Superintendent and innovation leader, I've seen first hand how transformative Career Technical Education can be when done with purpose and heart. This book is a practical and empowering resource for CTE teachers and any educator seeking to develop rigorous, student-centered programs that connect classroom learning to the real world. It's time we elevate CTE not just as an option, but as a cornerstone of 21st-century education."

– **Dr. Matthew X. Joseph**, *CEO of X-Factor EDU & Assistant Superintendent of Teaching and Learning in New Bedford MA*

"The weird and wonderful world of Career and Technical Education has been made more accessible and approachable through this book. Before becoming a CTE instructor, I was unaware of the impact and importance of this often-overlooked framework of education. This work shines a spotlight on CTE, elevating it to the recognition it merits in today's educational landscape."

– **Timothy Roden**, *CTE Educator in New Jersey*

"This book is a powerful guide for every CTE educator seeking to move beyond technical instruction and truly unlock student potential. By weaving together adolescent development, authentic learning experiences, and practical classroom strategies, it provides a roadmap that is both inspiring and actionable. It reminds us that preparing students for their careers also means preparing them for life—through reflection and real-world connections. A must-read for anyone committed to transforming CTE instruction into a catalyst for lasting student success."

– **Kevin J. Fleming**, *Ph.D., Author, Speaker, CEO of Catapult Masterclass*

# The Secondary Educator's CTE Toolkit

This book equips secondary Career and Technical Education (CTE) teachers with strategies and information to create rigorous, meaningful, and comprehensive CTE programs, supporting educators in traditional work-based learning programs as well as schools looking to infuse career programming into their curriculum. It is also designed to guide both teachers moving into CTE from other subject areas and industry professionals entering the field from an alternative certification program. Each chapter is infused with a myriad of strategies for teachers to make your classroom "career ready," drawing on 21st-century classroom curriculum design. Each topic introduced, from assessment, collaborating with community partners and school stakeholders, work-based experiences, and more, includes an introduction, several instructional suggestions, a "teacher spotlight" demonstrating the strategies in action, and discussion questions for individual or book study use. Sample lessons, projects, and interviews with experts supplement the chapters. Whether you're a current CTE teacher or just looking to infuse career-ready material into existing secondary curriculum, this resource can help you create meaningful CTE learning to prepare your students for their world after your classroom.

**Samantha Shane** is a Career and Technical Education (CTE) teacher in New Jersey and an ASCD Emerging Leader.

# Also Available from Routledge Eye on Education
(www.routledge.com/eyeoneducation)

Unlocking the Career and Technical Education Classroom:
Lessons for Real World Learning in Grades 6-12
Ashley Johnson

STEM Matters: Your Guide to Educational Purposes,
Policies, Programs, and Practices
Rodger W. Bybee, Patrick L. Brown

The Explore-Before-Explain Guidebook for Science Education:
Creating High Quality Lessons for the Classroom
and Professional Learning
Patrick L. Brown

Teaching STEAM Through Hands-On Crafts: Real-World
Maker Lessons for Grades 3-8
Christine G. Schnittka, Amanda Haynes

STEM by Design: Tools and Strategies to Help Students in
Grades 4-8 Solve Real-World Problems
Anne Jolly

Turning it Around: Small Steps or Sweeping Changes to
Create the School Your Students Deserve
Todd Whitaker, Courtney Monterecy

How to Get All Teachers to Become Like the Best Teachers
Todd Whitaker

Culturally Responsive and Sustaining Science Teaching:
Teacher Research and Investigation from Today's Classrooms
Elaine V. Howes, Jamie Wallace

STEAM Teaching and Learning Through the Arts and Design:
A Practical Guide for PK-12 Educators
Debrah C. Sickler-Voigt

# The Secondary Educator's CTE Toolkit

Igniting the Spark for Career Readiness in Your Classroom

Samantha Shane

Routledge
Taylor & Francis Group
NEW YORK AND LONDON

Designed cover image: © Getty Images

First published 2026
by Routledge
605 Third Avenue, New York, NY 10158

and by Routledge
4 Park Square, Milton Park, Abingdon, Oxon, OX14 4RN

*Routledge is an imprint of the Taylor & Francis Group, an informa business*

© 2026 Samantha Shane

The right of Samantha Shane to be identified as author of this work has been asserted in accordance with sections 77 and 78 of the Copyright, Designs and Patents Act 1988.

All rights reserved. The purchase of this copyright material confers the right on the purchasing institution to photocopy or download pages which bear the support material icon and a copyright line at the bottom of the page. No other parts of this book may be reprinted or reproduced or utilised in any form or by any electronic, mechanical, or other means, now known or hereafter invented, including photocopying and recording, or in any information storage or retrieval system, without permission in writing from the publishers.

For Product Safety Concerns and Information please contact our EU representative GPSR@taylorandfrancis.com. Taylor & Francis Verlag GmbH, Kaufingerstraße 24, 80331 München, Germany.

*Trademark notice*: Product or corporate names may be trademarks or registered trademarks, and are used only for identification and explanation without intent to infringe.

ISBN: 978-1-032-98314-1 (hbk)
ISBN: 978-1-032-98313-4 (pbk)
ISBN: 978-1-003-59805-3 (ebk)

DOI: 10.4324/9781003598053

Typeset in Palatino
by Newgen Publishing UK

Access the Support Material: www.routledge.com/9781032983134

# Contents

*Meet the Author* ........................................ viii
*Acknowledgments* ........................................ ix
*Online Support Materials* ............................. xii

Introduction ............................................. 1

1 Unlocking Student Potential ........................... 6

2 Theory Meets Practice ................................ 35

3 Creating Authentic Learning Experiences ............. 72

4 Work-Based Learning Experiences ..................... 98

5 Grading and Assessments in CTE ..................... 130

6 Guest Speakers and Collaborating with
  Stakeholders ....................................... 169

7 Working with Diverse Learners ...................... 193

8 The Power of Reflection ............................ 217

# Meet the Author

Samantha Shane is a Career Technical Educator from New Jersey who is passionate about making learning a tangible experience for her students. Her love for education began in her own high school years, when she attended a Career Technical School in northern New Jersey to study child-related careers. She went on to earn a bachelor's degree in English education from Montclair State University. Later, she earned her master's degree in curriculum and instruction from Caldwell University.

Samantha started her career as an English teacher at a Career Technical High School, where she discovered her passion for igniting a love of reading and writing in her students. She soon found herself drawn to working with other educators, discussing best practices, and shaping the future of education. This led her to a new opportunity: becoming a CTE teacher herself, working directly with high school students who aspire to become educators.

Today, Samantha focuses on crafting relevant and engaging CTE experiences that empower students to take ownership of their learning. She prioritizes student choice, ensuring that every lesson provides meaningful, real-world skills that prepare them for their chosen career paths. Her goal is to bridge the gap between theoretical knowledge and practical application.

# Acknowledgments

School and learning have given me so many opportunities, joy, love, and growth. I'm lucky to have a passion for learning. I could spend days brainstorming projects or looking at classroom setups. There is nothing more exciting than looking at a learning standard and thinking of the endless possibilities of student learning. This book is born out of a desire to help other teachers because so many educators have shaped my own journey. Being able to work with other passionate educators, attend high-quality conferences, and meet incredible educators continues to renew my own practice. They inspired me to pursue this career, try new things with each other, listen to my complaints when I have a bad day, and, most importantly, believe in me. Thank you to the reader for finishing this book and considering some new ideas. I know that change can be challenging, but I hope this book serves as a small encouragement to take a new step. It is in that pursuit of new possibilities that we truly ignite the fire of learning for our students – and for ourselves.

*To my family* who always listened to my endless list of things I wanted to accomplish and achieve. I appreciate all you have done to support me and always listen to my big dreams. Dad, Poppy, Nana, and Dylan, thank you for always being my number one fans. Mom, thank you for instilling in me the belief that there is nothing I can't accomplish if I set my mind to it.

*To Lisa Adams*, I didn't know when I was 15 years old how much your guidance would impact me. You have been a constant mentor and challenged me to learn, grow, and be better. Thank you for helping me become more confident and pursue every opportunity. I appreciate your willingness to always listen to my ideas, travel the United States for different conferences and always be honest with me.

*To Gina Visconti and Cathy Mohrle*, I am sincerely grateful for your friendship and support. I couldn't have completed this project without the both of you.

*To my coworkers and administration team*, I love being able to work in such an amazing place where I am supported, encouraged, and excited each day. Thank you for your unwavering support and the space for me to learn.

*To my students*, past, present, and future, thank you for filling my classroom with purpose and passion. The opportunity to plan, to provide opportunities, and to simply listen to your ideas has been my greatest reward. Seeing you grow and succeed is what inspires me to be better each day. I am so proud of your journey, and I hope you never stop learning.

*To future CTE educators*, I hope you fall in love with teaching as much as I did. Being able to work with students each day energizes me. I want to do better for them. I hope this book serves you well. Don't give up and find your reason for doing better each day. My own teaching journey has always been easy. When I first graduated college, I had a hard time finding a job. The market was scarce, and English teachers were a dime a dozen. I was able to secure a maternity leave position in a school district that was rough.

*To the team at Routledge and Julia Dolinger*, thank you for believing in me and answering my thousands of questions. I look forward to our partnership in the future.

*To other educators* that have impacted me throughout my career. Jennifer Skomial, Christine Hietanen, Melissa Conceicao, Nicole Couto, Nancy Kucinski, Dr. Joanne Jasmine, and many more. I'm lucky to have had strong educators that guided my journey and exposed me to many experiences. At each stage of my career, you have shaped me one way or another.

*To my friends*, thank you for always being supportive of my goals and listening to me talk about my dreams.

This book was born from the privilege of working with countless CTE teachers and witnessing firsthand their resilience in overcoming the many barriers of a career change. I have immense respect for anyone who leaves their industry to become an educator; your deep knowledge is the most powerful tool you bring to the classroom. The thoughts shared here are a reflection of my personal journey and extensive research, not a representation of any single institution. There is so much more on each of the topics covered. I hope you explore more resources and dive into a topic you are passionate about. I loved learning about the diverse CTE programs flourishing across the country, and I am excited for all the incredible things CTE will accomplish in the years to come.

# Online Support Materials

The CRP Task Cards in Chapter 5 can be accessed online by visiting this book's product page on our website: www.routledge.com/9781032983134 (then follow the links indicating Support Material, which you can then download directly).

# Introduction

How do educators prepare students for the world of tomorrow? How can teachers make the 8-hour school day meaningful to each student and give students the tools to be successful? Career Technical Education (CTE) provides students the opportunity to gain real world skills while in compulsory education. Forget everything you thought you knew about "vocational education". Today's CTE is not a fallback option; it is the strategic blueprint for the 21st-century workforce, directly shaping the innovators, problem-solvers, and essential professionals our world desperately needs. Over the past two decades, CTE has transformed the way educators are thinking about the purpose of schools. As a CTE teacher, administrator, or student reading this book, you know the importance of providing CTE classes to students. In 2023, 11.3 million students were engaged in CTE programs (Galvan, 2024). This number only continues to grow as CTE becomes more accessible to students. But with this core belief, what is the best way to teach content, practical skills, and professional? This book seeks to answer this question and provide strategies to use in the classroom to give students the best education possible and ultimately be successful in a job where things can be constantly changing.

The challenge of preparing students for the future is not a new one; it is a question that has evolved over the past century, beginning with the very foundation of CTE. The term "vocational education" was used for many years, but it often carried outdated perceptions and negative stereotypes about its purpose and rigor. The rebranding of the field to "CTE" was a deliberate effort to reflect the modern, academically rigorous, and holistic nature of today's programs, which are designed to prepare all students for both college and career. The Smith-Hughes Act of 1917 laid the foundation for funding for vocational education. It was the first federal funding for vocational education in the United States. After that, first several more acts provided funding for vocational education, specifically in the trades of agriculture, home economics, and trades (History – 100 Years of Advance CTE, n.d.). In the 1950s, the first major shift to expanding vocational education to cities was discussed. More interesting was the expansion of programs like laboratory technicians, junior chemists, and special industry equipment operators because of the Space Race between the United States and Soviet Union (History – 100 Years of Advance CTE, n.d.). President Johnson in the 1960s expanded vocational education even more by providing services to disadvantaged students and students with disabilities; he also signed amendments to further research and establish permanent programs. This led to national and state advisory councils and state plans that had procedures and annuals plans (History – 100 Years of Advance CTE, n.d.).

In 1983, A Nation at Risk was published. This led to Carl D. Perkin, a congressman and strong advocate for vocational education, creating a major shift in vocational education in 1984 and increased funding. The Perkins Act included a focus on guidance counseling, partnerships to meet the needs of high technology sectors, and program evaluation to measure impact. Over the years, Perkins Act Funding has been reauthorized to continue improving the quality of education and the link to post-secondary education. With each reauthorization, access and the concept of CTE were strengthened. The stigma around vocational education has existed for too long, and traditionally, many may think of CTE schools as vocational schools. Vocational schools offered traditional programs like carpentry, plumbing, electrical, cosmetology, and welding. Schools typically sent their "bad or misbehaved" students to these programs. CTE and vocational schools remained dedicated to providing students with hands-on experience that is preparing students for the world of tomorrow.

In 2006, the term "career and technical education" was used instead of vocational to reflect the changing idea of CTE (History – 100 Years of Advance CTE, n.d.). In the last reauthorization of Perkins in 2018, it made important updates, streamlined accountability measures, enhanced efforts to service special populations, and encouraged invocation. Perkins plays a critical role in providing key funding, improving the quality of CTE, and promoting innovation. Understanding the past history of CTE is important for the future. The history demonstrates how important CTE education has been since its inception.

Today, the Association for Career and Technical Education (ACTE) is the largest national education association dedicated to preparing students for careers. To help answer the question "what is high-quality CTE?", they created a framework for schools to use to model their programs. The framework is built around 12 essential elements and over 90 detailed criteria (High-Quality CTE Framework Development – ACTE Online, n.d.). Within each chapter, it will link to one or more of the 12 essential elements. The framework provides CTE teachers with a clear roadmap for creating learning experiences that prepare students for the future. More importantly, it helps us identify strengths and weaknesses of our programs. By understanding the framework, CTE teachers can move beyond simply teaching a subject to building a student-centered program.

My own experience in a CTE school started when I was an eighth grader. I grew up in a small town where students attended a neighboring high school. I remember sitting in our cafeterias/multiple purpose room listening to a speaker from the county CTE school telling us all about the programs offered. The thrill of working with preschool students and learning all about teaching seemed like a dream. Many other buzzwords like college preparation, technology, and rigor were also said, but I didn't fully understand them at the time. All I cared about was being able to work with children every day. My parents were wary at first about the idea but supported my decision to apply. Fast forward through an application process, interview, and acceptance, I was ready to gain hands-on experience and started my journey. During my 4 years in high school, I was able to teach in a preschool, learn important child development theories, understand how to lesson plan, and much more. I was more prepared to pinpoint that I wanted to work with high school students and not elementary age. This decision saved me thousands of dollars and my time in college. Once in college, I believe I had an edge on my peers just beginning to learn about educational theories and how to teach.

After I graduated high school and college, I had the opportunity to return to my CTE high school and teach English Language Arts (ELA). Teaching a core academic subject to students in all different types of CTE programs made me better understand the skills, concepts, and understandings that students needed to develop to be successful after high school graduation. It challenged my teaching to make ELA more relevant for the students and demonstrate the importance of these skills in their future careers. I loved being able to partner with a CTE teacher to make learning come alive as we fused our subjects together for a meaningful project. It also led me to working closely as an instructional coach with CTE teachers and understanding their struggles which were so unique to teachers in a traditional high school. Eventually, a CTE teaching position opened up, and I transitioned to working with high school students interested in the field of education. As a CTE teacher, I love being able to brainstorm hands-on, real-world opportunities for my students. My journey, much like many new CTE teachers, has been one of constant learning and adaptation in the dynamic world of vocational education. While I worked in a CTE high school as an English teacher, I was lost when it first came to understanding work-based learning experiences, industry-recognized credentials, and working with different stakeholders. This book is born from that experience – from the successes, the challenges, and the unwavering belief that every single student deserves a direct, relevant pathway to a fulfilling career.

The numbers are stark: countless industries face a widening skills gap, with millions of high-paying jobs going unfilled due to a lack of qualified talent. Meanwhile, many graduates struggle to bridge the gap between academic theory and workplace readiness. This urgent crisis demands a reimagining of education, a challenge that CTE is uniquely positioned to address head-on. I hope this book serves as a guide to help CTE educators create strong programs for their students. This book provides introductory information, and there aren't enough pages to cover everything. Each chapter has recommended books for those interested in taking a deeper dive. Additionally, you can find discussion questions to further guide your learning journey. When I first started teaching, my mentor once said something that stuck with me and I hope you remember as you read this book. Excellence is a journey, not a constant. Focus on one area per week: this week, lesson planning; next week, grading and feedback. You can't do it all, and you certainly won't be successful at every single thing. Take a risk, and be open to trying new things. I hope this advice serves you well like it has me.

## References

Galvan, J. (2024, September 20). *OCTAE Releases 2022-23 Perkins Enrollment and Performance Data*. CTE Policy Watch. Retrieved August 1, 2025. https://ctepolicywatch.acteonline.org/2024/09/octae-releases-2022-23-perkins-enrollment-and-performance-data.html

High-quality CTE Framework Development – ACTE Online. (n.d.). Association for Career and Technical Education. Retrieved July 31, 2025. www.acteonline.org/professional-development/high-quality-cte-tools/high-quality-cte-development/

History – 100 Years of Advance CTE. (n.d.). Advance CTE. Retrieved July 18, 2025. https://careertech.org/about/history/

# 1

# Unlocking Student Potential

Jimmy, a high school junior, was working on an old truck he wanted to use when he got his driver's license. Through this process, Jimmy was invested in understanding how the mechanics of each part worked to get it road-ready. When he finally got the truck running, through his tenacity and innate curiosity, the project ignited something inside of him. Jimmy told me that he always liked working with his hands. He loves being able to take things apart, understand how things work, and fix things. His mother, Cathy Mohrle, a high school English teacher, even chimed in, saying he had been doing this since he was two, when his grandmother found him underneath his pack and play with a screwdriver. He was trying to dismantle it.

Sitting down with Jimmy to discuss his reasons for enrolling in a CTE program, I was reminded of how exciting it is to think about the future and to take those initial steps. Jimmy has many strengths and is smart, but never had the desire to go to college. Many adults in his school push the academic career path of going to college; many teachers just assume college is the next step for students. For Jimmy, a traditional desk job and attending college are not in his future; he would much rather be out in the field, using his hands to solve problems. Luckily for students like Jimmy, his county CTE school was recruiting for the share-time programs they offered. At first, Jimmy thought the electrical trade was going to be his pathway. He said many adults were telling him that it was easy and he could make a ton of money. In the process of learning about applying and enrolling in the CTE school, he attended two information sessions at the school, career days at his high school, and a campus tour with the CTE school counselor. Through this process, Jimmy's dream was confirmed.

Ultimately, Jimmy enrolled in a plumbing and pipefitting course because he was inspired by the teacher's classroom. While his choice to enroll was easy, Jimmy has several obstacles to overcome. Jimmy attends his town's high school for his core academic classes and attends the county CTE high school for half the day. His typical day will include waking up early to get on a bus to his local high school, where he switches to a different bus to the CTE high school. After spending almost 3 hours in his CTE program, Jimmy will get on another bus to return to his home district. The timely commute is something Jimmy is willing to sacrifice to learn the trade and gain valuable, employable skills. Another obstacle Jimmy faces is the change in course load. At this home district, Jimmy cannot enroll in other electives that interest him since his CTE course fulfills his elective requirements. He feels that many academic teachers are unaware of his CTE schedule, and it would be beneficial to students if they did so they can make coursework relevant to them. He is also a football player whose sports schedule will be impacted. The CTE schedule ends later than his home district, so Jimmy will be late to football practice his senior year, and he won't be able to start work study until December, when the football season ends.

The plumbing and pipefitting course is all hands-on work, and Jimmy is excited to have a break from the monotony of traditional school. He's ready to disconnect from the screen and finally have "fun" at school. He is looking forward to meeting new people from other sending districts who share similar goals and a mindset. He knows how important this opportunity is and will take full advantage of it. He sees enrolling in this course as the equivalent of getting into college. It marks the beginning of his future.

Jimmy is not the only student who feels this way. In recent years, there has been a shift as fewer students are attending college in order to find fulfilling career pathways. The pressure to attend has increased in schools, but the enrollment in college has decreased over the past 10 years (National Center for Education Statistics, 2024). Generation Z (Gen Z) is born between 1997 and 2012 and will comprise 27% of the workforce at the end of 2025 (Kelly, 2025). What is interesting about Gen Z is their values-first mindset to work and desire to provide an impact. Gen Z is prioritizing working for organizations with strong ethical stances that reflect their own ideals (Kelly, 2025). How can our schools help prepare students who are demanding more for companies and pursuing passion instead of a paycheck?

CTE classes directly tap into the adolescent brain's drive for novelty and exploration. By offering hands-on experiences in diverse fields, these programs provide the perfect outlet for teens to try new things, discover hidden talents, and ignite a passion for learning. How you focus your attention during adolescence plays an important role in shaping the growth of your brain (Siegel, 2014, p. 82). The teen brain is wired for social connection, and CTE classes provide a built-in community for collaboration and mentorship. Working on real-world projects alongside peers fosters teamwork, communication, and a sense of belonging, all crucial for adolescent development. Adolescence is a time of heightened emotions, and CTE classes offer a healthy outlet for this energy. The thrill of mastering a new skill, the satisfaction of creating something tangible, and the pride of contributing to a team project can all provide powerful emotional rewards for teens. Whether it's designing a website, building a robot, or developing a marketing campaign, these programs empower teens to express their creativity, think outside the box, and find innovative solutions to real-world challenges. CTE classes are uniquely suited to the developing teen brain.

Teenagers think critically, share feelings, engage in reflection, and feel deeply about the world around them. I've seen the teenage brain wheels "spin" when students are reflecting or in a period of true growth. High school students can talk about hopes for the future, have discussions around current events, and should know right from wrong. There is a misconception that they should "know better" and are treated like adults in many situations. Understanding where high school students are in their development is important for building a successful CTE student and program. CTE teachers, who often focus on technical skills and career preparation, may overlook the crucial role of understanding adolescent development in maximizing student potential. I certainly overlooked how critical this piece was in understanding my students. Understanding this pivotal period can help teachers better create classrooms that curb misbehaviors and foster a thriving student environment. Depending on when students are eligible for a CTE program in their county, they may be entering the program as a new ninth-grade student or a 16-year-old junior. There are major differences in maturity and development between the grade levels. Understanding these differences may help when creating a new CTE program and what age students are able to participate in it.

In the book, *Brainstorm: The Power and Purpose of the Teenage Brain*, Daniel J. Siegel explains that teenagers often get a bad reputation as rebels, hormone-crazed, and immature. The teenage brain is going through the second most important period of growth (2014). Siegle dismantles the negative stereotypes of teenagers and demonstrates the importance of adolescence and addresses where teens are in their development. When teachers hold these negative ideas about students, studies show they perform worse (Siegel, 2014, p. 4). A largely accepted idea about teenagers is the idea that they push away from adults and authority. Looking at this idea from another perspective is that teenagers can help spark positive change, provide a new perspective, and push adults to innovate from the "norm". Teachers should lean into this notion of pushing away from the "norm" to have students create something new, problem solve, and ultimately become independent, adaptable, and innovative thinkers. By using the information about the teenage brain, educators can positively shape the growth of teens during this growth phase. Adolescence is marked by four prominent features of growth: a yearning to explore new experiences, a deep need for social connection, amplified emotional responses, and a blossoming of creative expression (Seigel, 2014, pp. 7–8). During the teen years, they show great emotional intensity, social engagement, and creativity (Siegel, 2014, p. 4). While it may seem like teenagers are just going through a phase, they are experiencing neurological changes driving the teen's brain development. When CTE teachers can tap into these drives, it fosters healthy development, encourages positive brain development, and channels the adolescent energy into something productive.

Emotions are not merely bystanders in the learning process; they are foundational drivers. Research shows that how a person "feels" about learning determines the amount of attention devoted to it (Sousa, 2022, p. 43). Since the brain's main job is to help humans survive, emotions play a role in memory and attention. For true learning to flourish, the educational environment must intentionally cultivate both physical safety and emotional security (Sousa, 2022, p. 42). Moreover, studies confirm that when students make a genuine emotional connection with subject matter through passion projects, real-world applications, or collaborative endeavors, their ability to recall curriculum content significantly increases (Sousa, 2022, p. 77). Tapping into a teenager's emotions combined with metacognition strategies can help increase learning opportunities. Fostering environments where students feel empowered to pursue projects they genuinely care about, where their creative impulses are celebrated and where resilience is built through safe exploration and the allowance for productive failure. Metacognition, the act of thinking about one's own thinking, becomes even more potent when infused with emotional awareness. Encouraging students to reflect not just on *what* they learned, but *how* they felt about the process, *why* they felt that way, and *how* those emotions impacted their problem-solving or retention deepens their understanding and self-regulation. For instance, after grappling with a complex CTE project, guiding students to articulate their frustration and then their satisfaction upon achieving a breakthrough reinforces the learning process and builds perseverance.

In CTE programs, where hands-on challenges can lead to both immense satisfaction and moments of intense frustration or self-doubt, acknowledging and addressing these emotional responses is vital. Creating space to celebrate small wins, validate struggles, and teach coping mechanisms for design failures or difficult technical tasks directly contributes to a resilient and engaged learner. Ultimately, understanding the intricate interplay between emotion, cognition, and the adolescent brain is not just a pedagogical phase; it is an imperative for creating powerful, memorable, and truly transformative learning experiences.

While the brain is continuing to develop, many physical changes are also happening, including growing taller, facial hair, and puberty. The brain continues to develop until a person reaches their mid-20s. The importance of providing students with opportunities to practice prioritizing and making good decisions is vital to their development. Teens are often faced with many challenges socially, including peer pressure, drugs, alcohol, vapes, and sex. Other challenges like familial problems, mental health issues, and eating disorders are often increased in teenagers. Teens become more independent and make choices that may impact their schooling. In teens, ages 12–14 (some ninth graders), students have more interest and influence from their peers, focus on themselves, going back and forth between high expectations and low confidence, experience more moodiness, and feel a lot of sadness, according to the Centers for Disease Control (CDC) milestones. For thinking and learning, this age group has more ability for complex thoughts, develops a strong sense of right and wrong, and expresses feelings through talking (Centers for Disease Control, 2024c).

In teens, ages 15–17 (the majority of high schoolers), students are developing their unique personality and finding out who they are. During this time, promoting a sense of independence and responsibility prepares them for future success. The emotional changes during this period of growth include: more interest in romantic relationships, a deeper capacity for caring, spending a lot of time with friends, and feelings of sadness. There is a large difference in mindset from a ninth grader to an eleventh grader. Some CTE programs strictly begin in junior year for this reason. These guidelines are important to know but aren't concrete. Students could be 16 but very immature. Each student will reach milestones at different times, and being encouraging and supportive through their development will contribute positively. Providing safe learning environments for students to take risks and learn from their mistakes can help develop teens.

---

**Key Takeaways**

- Meet students where they are.
- Tap into innate curiosity.
- Cultivate choice and personalize learning to fuel engagement.
- Foster an environment where learning from mistakes is industry standard.
- Integrate social connection and real-world relevance daily.

---

## Memory and the Brain

According to the Centers for Disease Control, during this age, teenagers learn more defined work habits, show more concern about future school and work plans, and can make their own choices. CTE programs support thinking and learning organically (Centers for Disease Control, 2024b. What is interesting is the research by the National Institute of Mental Health (NIMH), the prefrontal cortex is one of the last parts of the brain to mature. This part of the brain is responsible for skills like planning, prioritizing, and making good decisions (National Institute of Mental Health, 2023). As a teacher working with teens each day, it is easy to say "they are old enough to know better", but brain research says differently. How can teachers continue to support teenagers during this period of growth? We need to create an environment where students can have opportunities to practice planning, exercise time management, and plan for the future. First, creating relationships is foundational to the success of students. Showing interest outside the classroom creates a relationship and a trusted adult in the building. It helps promote an environment where teens can ask for help during planning or turn to a trusted adult when making a big decision. Acknowledging teenagers' successes, both in and out of the classroom, is crucial for building their self-esteem and motivation. Teenagers need someone they can turn to in case of hardship for support. Second, providing students with outlets to foster independence and creativity allows students to find themselves in a safe environment. Teaching students how to take risks and learn from mistakes supports teens turning into healthy adults.

As teachers, we hope students will remember the valuable content we teach each day. Students may seem to have a skill or knowledge today, but come to class the next day, forgetting it all. There are different stages and types of memory. Understanding the stages of memory can help teachers use research to plan brain-based lessons. First, short-term memory is the early stages of long-term memory and is related to immediate memory and working memory. Immediate memory is when we remember something for a few seconds. The most often used example of this is remembering a phone number to call someone, then forgetting it afterward. Working memory is when students build, take apart, or rework ideas for long-term memory (Sousa, 2022, p. 43). It was discovered that the brain can only handle a few items of working memory at a time. Recent research estimates that teenagers can handle three to five chunks of information at a time (Sousa, 2022, p. 44). In a CTE context, a "chunk" could be a specific safety procedure, a sequence of steps in a repair process, or the core function of a particular tool. To honor this capacity, teachers should break down complex tasks into manageable steps, focusing on a few key concepts or procedures at a time. Using clear visual aids, logical sequences, and frequent checks for understanding can help students effectively process and organize these chunks. Making content inherently related to prior knowledge and to each other, and presenting it in a logical, organized manner, significantly helps to store information efficiently and limit cognitive overload and confusion. For information to be truly consolidated into long-term memory, the brain essentially asks two critical questions: "Does this make sense?" and "Does this have meaning?" (Sousa, 2022, p. 48).

- Content makes sense when it is logically structured, clearly explained, and connected to existing knowledge. In CTE, this means demonstrating the *why* behind a procedure, explaining how different components of a system interact, or breaking down complex theories into practical, understandable applications. Analogies and cause-and-effect relationships are powerful tools here.
- Meaning is derived from personal relevance and real-world application. For CTE students, connecting curriculum to their career aspirations, future earnings, problem-solving real-world challenges, or contributing to their community provides immense meaning. Allowing students choice in projects, fostering collaboration, and linking learning to emotional experiences also deepen this meaning.

There have been many times when I thought my instruction was clear, and I would bet money that my students knew the information. To my surprise, students would claim "we didn't learn this" or "I don't remember". I usually took a deep breath before replying and telling students exactly when I taught them this information. Why couldn't my students remember anything I taught them? Understanding the "forgetting curve" is equally vital, research shows that the greatest loss of newly acquired information occurs within the first 18 to 24 hours (Sousa, 2022, p. 48). To combat the curve and ensure information makes the leap to long-term storage, CTE teachers can implement strategies such as:

- Immediate Review: A quick recap or "exit ticket" at the end of a lesson, asking students to summarize key takeaways or identify one concept they understood.
- Repetition and Retrieval: Briefly revisiting key concepts or skills across multiple days or weeks, rather than just once, can help students retain the information. This could involve "do now" questions, meaningful learning activities, review activities, or specific skill challenges.

- ♦ Active Application: The hands-on, project-based nature of CTE is inherently powerful for memory. Providing ample opportunities for students to *apply* their knowledge and skills through authentic tasks solidifies learning. When students actively do, build, diagnose, or create, they are engaging multiple sensory pathways and reinforcing neural connections.

I started repeating myself so much and consistently revisited concepts, ideas, and terms I wanted my students to absorb. To enhance student retention and embed valuable skills and knowledge for the long term, CTE educators must intentionally craft lessons that honor the brain's memory functions, from optimizing working memory intake to employing strategies for deep meaning-making and proactively countering the forgetting curve.

## The Brain and Thinking

What kind of thinking do we want our students to be engaging in? Are recalling facts and definitions important? Thinking is a complex process. As educators, we are constantly thinking, making decisions, and acting upon those thoughts. We want students to think critically about the work they are engaging in, but sometimes we are met with resistance from students. How can we begin to build thinking skills for students?

Handing students a variety of tools and saying go build a shed, give a haircut, or install a faucet wouldn't be the first thing you do in the classroom. Scaffolding, a term in education, refers to providing temporary support as students learn. The supports or scaffolds are taken away as students master the content. Thus, scaffolds serve as temporary measures to ensure the learning isn't too challenging, and students will shut down. In Lev Vygotsky's theory, he suggests that when learners are in the "Zone of Proximal Development", they can build on their previous knowledge and develop their skills (Bates, 2023, p. 48). CTE provides scaffolding as teachers introduce opportunities to work with different tools, practice various skills, and create different projects that help students learn their skills.

While relationships are foundational for building a culture of learning, talk is a powerful engagement tool. Studies show that talking about new learning helps the student to comprehend it and remember it (Sousa, 2022, p. 44). Thus, being purposeful in how we incorporate talking about learning can help students store information better. Second, teachers need to model thinking skills for students. Some examples of how teachers can do this are by the following (Sousa, 2022, p. 244):

- Showing interest in learning and committing to learning.
- Evaluating their own thinking process and explaining.
- Admitting mistakes.
- Giving students choice in their assignments.
- Providing opportunities for students to follow their own thinking.

While we typically want to separate emotions from learning, they are critical in the learning process. Research clearly demonstrates that positive emotions broaden a student's attention and enhance critical thinking, while negative emotions can constrict focus (Sousa, 2022, p. 240). Consequently, a teacher's genuine interest and visible commitment to a topic not only signal its importance but also transmit a positive emotional resonance to students. Conversely, when educators admit a topic isn't their favorite or label a chapter as "boring", even if attempting to build rapport, they inadvertently permit students to disengage. This seemingly harmless comment can significantly undermine student motivation and attention. Instead, even when faced with less personally engaging material, teachers should strive to find unique points of interest, explore challenging questions, or connect the content to broader, more exciting themes to model genuine curiosity and maintain an emotionally positive learning environment.

Multitasking while paying attention is a misconception in education. Research shows that while the brain can multitask in certain areas, like walking and talking, the ability to pay attention and multitask is a myth (Medina, 2008, p. 115). The brain processes things in a sequential order, making it impossible to carry out two cognitive processes simultaneously (Sousa, 2022, p. 28). We often mistake multitasking for task switching, where we move from doing one task to a different task and then returning to the original task (Sousa, 2022, pp. 28–29). For CTE teachers aiming to maximize student learning and skill acquisition, understanding these cognitive limitations is paramount. When students are preparing to engage with the day's learning activities, teachers should proactively structure the environment to minimize distractions and encourage focused attention. This involves clearly communicating expectations regarding materials, technology, and behavior before instruction begins. Having a clear structure of class, including a "do now", focuses students. Be aware of minimizing visual and auditory distractions. Model the behavior you want from students. Consider tech-free zones or times in the classroom. If students are using power tools, their cell phones need to be away. Establishing these clear expectations helps students thrive. When assigning complex activities, break them down for students.

## The Brain and Movement

My students have a love–hate relationship with moving while learning. First block begins at 8 a.m. and students stumble in to lie their head on their desk and wait for the day to begin. After morning announcements, I say the magic words, and students begin to groan: "Students, please stand up". These four words led to complaining as they slowly stood up. Ten minutes into the activity, students were buzzing with excitement, forgetting how sleepy they were moments ago. In one recent study, researchers found that parts of the brain that control movement relate to networks involved in thinking and planning (National Science Foundation, 2023). Movement plays a large role in our learning, and school is no longer done from just sitting at a desk.

When students are in a shop, they are standing at their workstation, and their whole body is engaged in the learning process. In other programs where students are sitting, think about how you can have students move more. Students moving in the classroom doesn't equal chaos. Short movement activities allow students to have an increase in oxygen. Consider the dynamic of a vocational shop class: students are constantly on their feet, standing at their workstation, and their whole body is engaged in the learning process as they manipulate tools and materials. This inherent physical activity supports deep, embodied learning. In other programs where students are predominantly sitting, it becomes crucial to intentionally design opportunities for movement.

## Building a Culture of Learning

Every class, every single day, I greet my students at the door. I say hello, hi, good morning, good afternoon, how are you, how was your game, or something to each of my students as they enter the classroom. As soon as the bell rings, I stop whatever I am doing to go greet my students. This small act cheers me up and shows my students I am excited about their learning and that each one of them belongs in our classroom. I also learn small things from my students during these moments. I've learned about their friends, often becoming acquainted with them as the year goes on. I've learned that if someone is in a bad mood and needs extra support. Being the friendly adult face in the hallway organically builds relationships. As you read this section, consider the following questions:

- ♦ What are my current beliefs about classroom management?
- ♦ What are my educational values?
- ♦ How do I want students to feel when they are inside my classroom?
- ♦ What procedures, rules, and routines are non-negotiable in my classroom?

As educators, we strive to be proactive instead of reactive. We hope that the rules, procedures, and systems we put in place are enough. At the core of a strong classroom and students' "doing", the work are strong relationships. Building these strong relationships takes time to develop. Students need to feel like they belong and are "safe" in the classroom. A widely accepted theory of behavior is Maslow's Hierarchy of Needs (1954). Abraham Maslow created a pyramid to show his theory of what motivates humans. At the bottom of the pyramid are basic physiological needs being met, like food, water, and sleep. The next level is safety, then love and belonging, then esteem, with the top of the pyramid being self-actualization. Educators today use Maslow's pyramid as a foundation for their classroom management. If our students don't have their most basic needs met, how can they fully reach their potential in the classroom? As teachers, we can control what happens inside our classrooms. We are charged with making a safe classroom environment, making students feel like they belong, and teaching students knowledge for the future. Thus, building strong relationships is important to building a robust classroom environment. Creating a classroom community that involves students in the process can lead to decreased behavior problems and increased motivation. This prevents numerous classroom challenges. At the beginning of the year, putting in the time to lay the groundwork is important and will lead to bigger gains in learning content later.

The first few weeks of school are important for creating a thriving classroom. Teachers may feel the pressure of getting through content, but by meticulously focusing on building a learning classroom, teaching content goes faster and students can find deeper meaning. Start with a student interest survey. The first day of school is the optimal time to get students excited about the program and introduce them to the classroom. I recommend planning an engaging activity that introduces skills, small amounts of content, and has students interacting with each other. I wait to introduce the syllabus to students until day 3 or day 4.

On the second day of school, I give students a series of pre-assessments to measure their skills. When I first started giving a pre-assessment, I spent hours grading them and gathering data on my students. I even created a chart with different points used when I was planning. However, the students never went back to that assignment. I give students an assessment that they will have to go back and revise. The initial assessment still gives me a ton of data to use, and students are still working on something that is meaningful. I have students create a lesson plan for a preschool classroom. This assignment gives me insight to their critical thinking and planning skills. After, I give them feedback and a series of workshops on lesson planning. Students will then revise the assignment, turn it in, and teach it to a group of preschool students. I also give students an interest survey. This survey can serve as an important tool to better understand how your students learn, their interests, and what students have going on outside the classroom. The survey will include questions like:

- What types of projects do you like to complete?
- Do you speak another language?
- Do you have commitments outside of school? If so, what are they?
- What other information do you think I should know?

I love reading the different survey answers, and more importantly, I gain insight. Students have shared sensitive information on these surveys that they might not have felt comfortable sharing face-to-face. It is critical to review the surveys in a timely manner in case students put sensitive information that needs to be dealt with, for example, mental health issues, unsafe living conditions, or abuse.

Additional tasks during the first weeks include setting up the classroom/shop, goal setting, going over shop safety, and mini-competitions. Mini-competitions can be timed problem-solving challenges, design sprints, or drills. I then involve students in the process of creating procedures. Students have chosen to attend your CTE class, and the first few weeks serve as an opportunity to demonstrate why students made the right choice. More importantly, it builds community and creates a culture of learning.

When I am ready to introduce the syllabus, I include students in the process. I have students co-create expectations in the classroom. When co-creating expectations, allow students to think of consequences. Make a list of safety issues that may happen for students to solve. Students can start to work through seeing different issues that could arise with tools and understand how important the safety regulations they need to follow. After, have the students summarize their takeaways and create a set of classroom rules. Allow students to create a class poster and hang it in the classroom or shop to serve as a constant reminder. In having these discussions, you can gain insight into the student thought process, clear up misconceptions, and be clear in expectations. It may seem elementary, but teach students how you want them to move desks when working in groups, individual work, and even cleaning up. In a shop setting, go over safety instructions and provide students the opportunity to practice the safety steps. Continuing to hold students to those expectations is critical for their development and the classroom culture. If there is an issue with student safety, pulling students aside to have a conversation is important to keep the student safe. It also helps to stop behaviors from progressing. I always require my students to get a parent's or guardian's signature stating they have read the rules.

Unfortunately, students will make mistakes, break rules, and misbehave. A few years ago, I had a student who would do something each time he walked into class. He would run and jump over chairs, swing his keys into the lights, or make ridiculous statements. Each time he would do something, it took a lot of patience not to get upset. I also felt like a failure as a teacher. As I tried to build a rapport with this student, I felt annoyed by his actions and failed to engage him. Of course, there were consequences to his actions, and he was trying to challenge me. As educators, we must respond in a way that supports their learning and growth. Teaching sometimes is personal for us, and we have preconceived ideas about students. As educators, we take pride in our lessons and care deeply about our work. However, students bring emotional baggage from another class, their home lives, and social lives into the classroom. Cell phones increase students' constant access to their friends and drama. Students will challenge the teacher and try to get away with certain behaviors. Taking the time to understand how to manage behavior and develop your own classroom management style is important. We cannot take this personally and be upset with the student. Take time before responding to a student who may be getting under your skin.

Some behaviors stem from learned behaviors in prior grades, social struggles, or a lack of support. Students with attention-deficit/hyperactivity disorder (ADHD), learning disabilities, and emotional struggles should not be automatically labeled as "bad students" or prejudged by their diagnosis. Each student, regardless of label or no label, should be treated with respect. Common complaints of student behavior for all students include cheating on assignments (copying from other students/using artificial intelligence (AI)/or taking from the internet), inappropriate comments, inappropriate use of tools, and putting down others. Each student and situation may have a different approach. Additionally, every school has its own expectations of behavior. Familiarizing oneself with the school rules, expectations, and procedures will help build a strong classroom management system.

Being clear about expectations and procedures you want in your classroom is important. Do you want student cell phones collected? Do you want students to take their smart watches off? Are certain shoes required to be in the shop? Being firm with the procedures and holding students accountable is important. In a recent meeting, our Student Resource Office (SRO) said a fake iPhone was turned in to his office. By turning in the fake cell phone, the student was able to try and use their cell phone. The student may not have even used it during the class, but the feeling of needing the cell phone on them led them to turning in a fake phone. Students will go to great lengths to have their phone or "get away" with not following the procedure.

One question that has started numerous student conversations when students are misbehaving is "Are you okay?". This question shifts the tone of the conversation and allows the student to share and approach the conversation reflectively. It also allows students to share if something is going on. Misbehaving can be a sign of something larger going on in a student's life. Students are sometimes silent when I first ask, and I give them time to talk. I wait several minutes before having a follow-up comment. This is when I say, " I noticed ... and wanted to make sure you are okay". Many students will start to explain, and this is where the real conversation happens. Addressing student behavior needs to happen quickly and swiftly. I even ask the question when I know the student did something. I always want my students to know they can own up to their mistakes. They will face the consequences, but this single question creates a relationship and acknowledges a student.

| Things to do | Things not to do |
|---|---|
| ♦ Pull your student aside for a conversation<br>♦ Follow up with an email<br>　♦ Copy the school counselor and/or parents<br>♦ Talk calmly and listen to students<br>♦ Treat each class as a new opportunity for students | ♦ Shame or humiliate students publicly or individually<br>♦ Yell at students<br>♦ Share student discipline with other students or other parents<br>♦ Hold a grudge against a student<br>♦ Escalate situations |

A common practice for student behavior/discipline is taking away something from students or rewarding students for their behavior. Punishments like taking away shop time, putting students' names on the board, or losing privileges to certain tools/projects may seem easy to implement and feel like students are being held accountable, but they may do more harm. Students become mad at the adult punishing them instead of reflecting on their actions, which creates tension that stays in the classroom (Smith et al., 2015, p. 9). Students might continue the behavior, further plotting how to get away with it in the future (Smith et al., 2015, p. 9). Punishments also reinforce the idea that this is the only way someone with power can get what they want (Smith et al., 2015, p. 9). Rewards shouldn't solely rely on behavior. So, carefully planning how to prevent behaviors will transform the classroom and minimize behaviors. Understanding the ABCs of behaviors helps. The A stands for antecedent, which is the event that triggers a certain behavior, the B stands for the behavior, and C is the consequences of the behavior (Smith et al., 2015,

p. 67). It is impossible to take the time and understand the ABCs of each student's behavior. However, this can help with students who constantly have a problem understanding their behavior. For these more challenging students, keep a document to record their behaviors. This informal data can help create a strong plan for students. It can also expose a larger problem the student is having. In certain situations, a behavior plan is developed with the parent, student, school leadership, and teacher. Within the behavior plan can be goals for the students and consequences. Restorative justice practices have seen greater results for increasing positive student behavior and decreasing negative student behavior. Consider how you are going to foster a classroom that challenges students to think critically, develop self-respect, nurture their creativity, and help students reach their goals.

Beyond classroom behaviors, something larger may be happening to your student. Students can be grappling with changing schools, the transition from their town's district where they knew everyone to a CTE high school can be overwhelming. Beyond a transitional change, students face peer pressure. Students might start experimenting with drinking and drugs. If you suspect a student is using drugs or alcohol, review your school's policies and procedures. It is not your job to investigate if a student is under the influence. Notifying the correct people in the building will ensure the child's health and safety. If a student makes a comment, joke, or statement about drugs or alcohol, report it. It may be uncomfortable, you think it is a joke, or you may not want to upset the student, but for the student's well-being, it's crucial to follow established protocols. Ignoring such statements, even if seemingly innocuous, could mean missing a cry for help or a sign of deeper issues. Your report allows trained professionals to assess the situation, provide support, and connect the student with necessary resources. It also shows the student the seriousness of the comments they make. In talking to the student, never accuse the student, search the student, or touch the student.

Students are also facing various medical diagnoses. As of 2025, 31.9% of teens have anxiety (NIMH) and 11% of teens have ADHD (Centers for Disease Control, 2024a). Supporting our teens through their various health issues and identifying the causes of some behaviors help support students. Having strong communication with the student, parents, and guidance counselor creates a strong team for the student. Unfortunately, some students have severe health issues that might cause them to be placed on home instruction. Many common issues may arise and affect teens, which can impact their learning and attendance in class.

Home instruction is when students receive their schoolwork through a teacher assigned by the school. Home instruction happens for a variety of reasons, when a student has a long-term issue, they need to be at home for. This often happens when a student needs surgery, inpatient or outpatient mental health services, and/or safety concerns. The assigned teacher will communicate with the student's teachers, parents, and students. Depending on the school and situation, home instructions will meet with the students for several hours. Assigning work to a student on home instruction for the CTE class can be challenging. When thinking about what work to assign, you can ask the counselor or home instructor if the student has any physical limitations or screen time restrictions. Sending home materials can be an option for students.

## School Roles to Help Support Students

In the school setting, there are many support systems that are in place to help students when they are in need. Knowing the different roles is essential to knowing which professional to partner with on different issues. As a teacher, while it may feel it is your job to take on the emotional burden and well-being of students, taking on this role can lead to teacher burnout and not help the students. Notifying and partnering with the right school personnel will make the biggest difference in helping a child. Being transparent and open with the trained professionals to handle situations and share confidential information is critical, and it also protects the teacher from consequences. Each school, district, and state is dependent on the school's philosophy, demographics, size, and overall culture. On the district website or staff handbook, roles should be clearly defined.

## Building Principal

Their multifaceted role encompasses the day-to-day operational management of the building, ensuring a safe, effective, and conducive learning environment. Beyond basic administration, building principals are instrumental in shaping the school's educational vision and culture. They also drive the implementation of curriculum initiatives, develop strategic plans to enhance student achievement, and launch educational programs. The building principal will update the superintendent on the school and staff.

## Assistant/Vice Principal

Each school may use the title of Assistant Principal or Vice Principal interchangeably. In most schools, assistant principals have designated duties. They will be charged with student discipline, supervising student activities, overseeing different departments, or professional development. Some assistant principals are your direct supervisor. Working with the assistant principal, if they are the disciplinarian, can help shape the classroom. Some teachers may have a stigma about working closely with an administrator and fear it could show a lack of confidence in how to be a teacher. Most administrators want to partner with teachers and provide support. The first step before contacting the assistant principal/disciplinarian is contacting the home if the offense isn't harming other students or the property of the school. Documentation of behaviors and contacting home is essential in showing the patterns of behavior and support for the student. Behavior contracts can be created, and in place, the assistant principal is involved.

## Instructional Coach

Students come into classrooms with different needs, knowledge, and ideas. Accessing an instructional coach, if a school has one, can provide instructional strategies that can boost student engagement. An instructional coach can offer a new way of teaching a concept, feedback on a lesson that isn't quite working right, or model a new instructional strategy. Providing instructional coaches with information about the current unit and students in the class can help make the time purposeful. Accessing instructional coaches takes the pressure or shame away from asking for help. Instructional coaches are not administrators, so being open and honest about needing help can improve outcomes in the classroom. It is important to be specific about what you would like to focus on with the instructional coach.

## School Counselor

Each student has an assigned school counselor who oversees students throughout their high school career. They are usually the first contact for parents and students when discussing postgraduate plans, struggles in classes, and mental health issues. School counselors have additional information and access to a student's history. A school counselor can also ask for feedback from other teachers to gain a better picture of a student if they are struggling. They will provide guidance to students about what courses to take and help give strategies for completing schoolwork. School counselors also help navigate social challenges with students.

There are many times to reach out to a school counselor. This includes the following: when a student is failing, has social issues, and is constantly getting in trouble. While the counselor is not the disciplinarian, they can help the student navigate emotional issues and understand the underlying cause. Teachers should always email home when students are failing and bcc the school counselor to keep them informed.

## Student Assistance Counselor

While the school counselor guides students on a variety of issues, the school assistance counselor offers a wider variety of confidential school-based services. This includes counseling, mental health assessments, crisis intervention, substance abuse prevention, and personal difficulties.

## School Social Worker

These mental health professionals focus on providing services related to a student's social, emotional, and academic life in school. They take on a unique role, like participating in special education assessments, Individual Education Plan (IEP) meetings, providing crisis intervention, developing strategies to increase academic success, helping students with social interaction, assisting with conflict resolution, and collaborating with parents and staff (School Social Work Association of America, n.d.). School social workers can help provide staff with essential information to help support a student, develop educational programs for students, provide case management, and advocate for new services for students (School Social Work Association of America, n.d.).

## Child Study Team (CST)

Each state has its own requirements about who sits on the child study team. This team includes the Learning Disabilities Teacher-Consultant, School Psychologist, and School Social Worker. This team is charged with evaluations when a student is referred for services, consulting on cases for students struggling, and coordinating services.

## Student Resource Officer (SRO)

In recent years, the role of the SRO has expanded in the public school system. A collaboration between the community's law enforcement and schools, a police officer is assigned as the SRO as a liaison between the school and law enforcement. The SRO's focus is to cultivate strong community ties, dispel law enforcement stereotypes, and work with the school to provide a safe environment for students. SROs might host programming in the school, like when students begin to drive. They might also assist when more serious crimes take place on campus. When dealing with different student issues, always call your school's administration before the SRO. The administration will call the SRO if necessary. SROs, since they are fully employed police officers, have to follow specific protocol for students.

## Communication

The family school connection is often neglected when students enter high school. The argument is that high school students should learn how to advocate for themselves and be responsible. The idea of students learning how to advocate for themselves and be accountable for their actions is critical, but family involvement can also be included. Connecting with home throughout a high school student's career strengthens a student's success. It can help support the whole child's development. One simple way I connect with home is by emailing something positive to the student and copying the parents. This notion of emailing the student and copying parents can be used for behavior or academic issues that arise. The following is an example email similar to something I've sent to students and copied their parents.

| To | studenta@CTEschool.org |
|---|---|
| Cc | parenta@email.com |

| Bcc | Person |
|---|---|
| **Subject** | Great Job Today! |

Good afternoon,

Thank you so much for planning and teaching all week! The preschoolers and preschool teachers enjoyed each lesson throughout the week. Each lesson was well-prepared, age- age-appropriate, and engaging. Your group dynamic complemented each other's strengths. The new preschool supervisor even complimented how professional and awesome you were. Thank you again, and enjoy the weekend.

Best,

Teacher Name

This email is simple and specific, which makes it timely for the students. There are times that warrant a phone call over email. Calling a parent may seem daunting, and many teachers become nervous when contacting home. However, calling home and talking to a parent can better help a student and foster a positive, supportive relationship. Speaking with a parent over the phone can clear up misunderstandings that could happen over email. Sometimes, words get misinterpreted, and people might read the tone wrong. A phone call is always appreciated and can quickly resolve an issue. After calling a parent, follow-up with an email summarizing the phone call. It may seem redundant, but it serves two purposes. First, it demonstrates a sense of caring about the student's well-being. Second, the conversation is documented, which can be evidence to show a supervisor or principal if the behavior continues.

Back-to-School Night is an important night for parents to connect with the educators their child will be with over the school year. This annual event is the opportunity for parents to immerse themselves in the classroom and gain insight into their child's curriculum. As an educator, making a good impression on this night is critical. Parents will be able to understand the teacher's personality, become familiar with class expectations, and envision the engaging and effective teaching methods that will be employed. As a result of this night, the school is able to gain the parents' confidence in the learning environment being provided to their child. Each school has its timeline for Back-to-School Night; knowing how long you have with parents is the first step to planning a successful event. A teacher's genuine self fosters trust and rapport with parents throughout the night. There are many different ways to present information to parents. The first option is a slideshow. Slideshows allow the teacher to break up the information into manageable chunks, allowing parents to digest the information. Teachers who might be nervous about presenting can rely on the slideshow to help them remember information. Another option is a handout for parents. The handout can include information about the course curriculum, important dates and links, contact information, and required materials. A handout ensures parents will have a copy of the information to take with them. Next, a teacher can choose to mimic hands-on learning with the parents. Teachers can have parents use the tools students engage with, try solving a challenging problem, or create something from materials in the classroom. Since time is usually limited, planning something meaningfully is important. Consider what information is critical for parents to hear and know when they are in the classroom or shop. Ultimately, parents want to leave Back-to-School Night with a clear sense of their child's educator, the classroom norms, and the intended learning outcomes. After Back-to-School Night is over, sending an email with the handouts, slideshow, or summary to all parents continues to build the support system. Parents appreciate the communication and information.

    The journey through the teenage years is a profound transformation. Being an educator working with teens for multiple years makes the journey a rewarding process. Jimmy plans on pursuing a full-time job with a major company while pursuing his plumbing license. He hopes to work for a large corporation or a water department where he will have full benefits and a retirement plan. He knows how important the next 2 years of high school are and will enjoy exploring the various careers within the plumbing and pipefitting trade. His advice for teachers is not to discount CTE for students or treat students differently. CTE courses, especially the trades, have a negative stigma that they are just for the "bad or stupid" kids. The trades are an extremely viable and necessary career field. During his senior year, he is required to pursue the Work-Based Learning (WBL) opportunity. He needs to be in good academic standing, have good attendance (no more than three absences), and be recommended by his CTE teacher to be eligible. The WBL opportunity allows Jimmy to work for a local plumbing company instead of attending class. He can go out 2 to 3 days a week and even earn a paycheck while doing it. If he ever changes his mind about plumbing after he finishes the program, he will have learned a valuable set of skills that can transfer into other fields. He encourages other students to take the chance and not to count anything out. Explore every option and be open to all different pathways.

Recognizing the natural drives for social connection, creative expression, and amplified learning is powerful indicators to fuel learning for students. Each educator is dedicated to the growth and success of students as they move to the next phase of their lives. By intentionally designing classroom environments that prioritize emotional safety, foster critical thinking, and encourage self-respect, educators can navigate common behavior issues and tap into the potential of reaching students. Using this information can effectively help unlock student potential.

 **Recommended Reading**

- *How the Brain Learns* by David Sousa.
- *Brainstorm: The Power and Purpose of the Teenage Brain* by David J. Siegel.

 **Discussion Questions**

- What biases and misconceptions do I hold regarding teenagers and their behaviors?
- What are the most prevalent challenges I observe in teens, and how can I leverage this information?
- What are the essential values as an educator that are important to include in designing a powerful classroom space?
- How can I create a culture that encourages and celebrates expression, rather than stifling it?
- Who are the key support personnel at my school, and how will I build relationships with them?

## References

Bates, B. (2023). *Learning Theories Simplified: ... and How to Apply Them to Teaching*. SAGE.

Centers for Disease Control. (2024a, November 19). *Data and Statistics on ADHD*. Centers for Disease Control and Prevention. www.cdc.gov/adhd/data/index.html

Centers for Disease Control. (2024b, May 16). *Positive Parenting Tips: Adolescence (15–17 Years Old)*. Centers for Disease Control and Prevention. www.cdc.gov/child-development/positive-parenting-tips/adolescence-15-17-years.html

Centers for Disease Control. (2024c, May 16). *Positive Parenting Tips: Young Teens (12–14 Years Old)*. Centers for Disease Control and Prevention. www.cdc.gov/child-development/positive-parenting-tips/young-teens-12-14-years.html

Kelly, J. (2025, April 1). *Gen-Z's Are Redefining the Way They Want to Work*. Forbes. Retrieved July 31, 2025. www.forbes.com/sites/jackkelly/2025/04/01/gen-zs-takeover-and-redefining-the-workplace/

Maslow, A. H. (1954). *Motivation and Personality*. Harper and Row.

Medina, J. (2008). Brain Rules. Pear Press.

National Center for Education Statistics. (2024, May). *College Enrollment Rates*. National Center for Education Statistics (NCES). Retrieved July 23, 2025. https://nces.ed.gov/programs/coe/indicator/cpb/college-enrollment-rate

National Institute of Mental Health. (2023). *The Teen Brain: 7 Things to Know*. National Institute of Mental Health. www.nimh.nih.gov/health/publications/the-teen-brain-7-things-to-know

National Institute of Mental Health. (n.d.). *Any Anxiety Disorder*. National Institute of Mental Health. www.nimh.nih.gov/health/statistics/any-anxiety-disorder

National Science Foundation. (2023, May 23). *Mind-Body Connection Is Built into Brain, Study Suggests*. NSF. Retrieved July 21, 2025. www.nsf.gov/news/mind-body-connection-built-brain-study-suggests

School Social Work Association of America. (n.d.). *Role of School Social Worker*. www.sswaa.org/school-social-work

Siegel, D. J. (2014). *Brainstorm: The Power and Purpose of the Teenage Brain*. Jeremy P. Tarcher/Penguin, a member of Penguin Group (USA).

Sousa, D. A. (2022). *How the Brain Learns* (6th ed.). Corwin.

Smith, D., Fisher, D., & Frey, N. (2015). *Better Than Carrots or Sticks: Restorative Practices for Positive Classroom Management*. Association for Supervision and Curriculum Development.

# 2

# Theory Meets Practice

Open the textbook to page 357 and complete questions 1–10 for class today. Define the 10 words and create sentences for the vocabulary. These are assignments I've assigned as a teacher. My students often silently roll their eyes, sneak a glance at a friend, or let out a loud sigh. I used to see these assignments as a necessary evil. Students needed to have the knowledge and content before I introduced a hands-on project. These are often traditional assignments teachers give students to learn content from a textbook. Textbooks, digital or hard copy, remain to be a staple in education. Teachers rely on textbooks for student-friendly content that is organized and ready to use. Teachers habitually default to textbooks, drawn by their structured curriculum and convenient implementation. More importantly, students need to have strong content knowledge before working with tools, interacting with industry partners, or taking on leadership roles. Textbooks help bridge the gap of knowledge, so students can work hands-on. How can teachers move beyond textbook learning to teach important knowledge, concepts, and ideas to move toward the hands-on parts of CTE programs? Where does a teacher begin when planning a lesson while using the textbook to teach important concepts?

Understanding how students, teachers, parents, and schools think matters most in planning and understanding how to create better lessons (Hattie, 2023, p. 7). Teachers, students, and parents all have preconceived ideas about what makes a good teacher, good lesson, and good school. School takes place during the most developmentally important milestones in our lives. In *Visible Learning: The Sequel,* Hattie (2023) draws on 2,100 meta-analyses and 130,000 studies to make conclusions about what we can improve in our schools and what actually does matter in schools. In looking at all his data, there is a conclusion about certain beliefs in education that emerge. First, the role teachers play in learning is large. Teachers truly do shape if students learn and grow. It was discovered that true learning is trial and error; building this into the curriculum can help students become more successful (Hattie, 2023, p. 120). More importantly, the role of the teacher is to know where each student is, where they need to be, and how to bridge that gap (Hattie, 2023, p. 120). Teachers having high expectations for their students was proven to have a large impact on student achievement (Hattie, 2023, p. 241). So what does this mean for planning in the classroom? It begins with careful planning by teachers to incorporate hands-on learning and opportunities for students to take risks. Students need to learn how to fail, pick themselves up, and try again.

Lesson planning is a common complaint by teachers but an integral part of planning rigorous student experiences that are strongly developed and focus on student learning. Lesson plans serve as a blueprint for teachers to use as they plan. Teaching is similar to building a house. You need to understand what the end product is going to look like, so building a strong blueprint for each involved member is important. Next, selecting materials for building a house is much like instructional strategies. There are many to choose from and some work better with others. While schools require different levels of lesson plans or no lesson plans at all, understanding how to properly plan for student learning will ultimately lead to better student outcomes, as it ensures that instruction is purposeful, engaging, and aligned with learning goals. Each teacher engages in some type of planning and has their own method. Some strategies that help lesson planning include printing out a calendar (monthly or weekly) to plan out each day. The first part of lesson planning is identifying learning standards. Standards allow teachers to make easier decisions on what to teach, assess, and lesson plan for each year. CTE programs each have standards that guide instruction. Standards are high-quality benchmarks that students need to reach to graduate and master a certain industry. It is important to check with your state's Department of Education for the standards. Advance CTE provides a nationally recognized framework that provides structure alignment on careers for states to use. The framework builds a bridge between work and school to give common language, build consistency, and ensure high-quality programs (Advance CTE, 2025). The Advance CTE Framework has 14 clusters and 72 sub-clusters. The clusters are based on the industry sectors defined by the Standard Occupational Classification and North American Industry Classification System codes (Advance CTE, 2025). At the core of the framework are career-ready practices. These are general professional skills that students need to be successful in any industry. Overall, using the framework can help guide curriculum writing, course sequencing, and reflects current industry trends.

Standards are learning expectations that students should know and be able to do by the end of a CTE program. Educators can think of them as benchmarks to learning and being successful in the industry. In traditional classes like math, English, science, and physical education, standards start in kindergarten, building on each other until students graduate from twelfth grade. Similarly, CTE programs have standards that help mirror foundational industry knowledge. The Common Core Technical Core is a set of high-quality standards for CTE programs that correspond to each of the 16 Career Clusters. Identifying what set of standards to use for your CTE program is important. Look to your school administration and state's Department of Education. Once your standards are identified, being able to unpack standards to understand them is an essential skill for setting students up for success.

In many instances, schools hire the teachers to write the curriculum for the program. Understanding by Design (UbD) is a framework for teachers to think purposefully of their curriculum planning (JDEC, n.d.). The goals of UbD are student understanding and the ability to transfer their learning. A unit plan includes these categories include:

- ◆ Stage 1: Desired Results
  At this stage, the teacher identifies the standards and thinks about the goals of the unit. Why are students learning this? Within Stage 1 are essential questions and enduring understandings that serve as a way to investigate the standards and raise important questions for learning (McTighe) (JDEC, n.d.). It also outlines the knowledge and skills students will learn as a result of this unit.
- ◆ Stage 2: Evidence
  During Stage 2 planning, the focus is on how we assess the learning from Stage 1. This includes the performance task at the end of the unit and other assessments that will help evaluate student learning. The key is to design the assessments before planning the lessons, ensuring that your evaluation methods are directly aligned with the desired results from Stage 1 (JDEC, n.d.).
- ◆ Stage 3: Learning Plan
  This final stage is where you design the actual lessons and activities (JDEC, n.d.). The focus here is on ensuring that what you teach and how you teach it directly aligns with the goals set in Stage 1 and prepares students for the assessments outlined in Stage 2. This is where you create the day-to-day instructional plan, designing a sequence of lessons that will help students acquire the necessary knowledge, practice the required skills, and ultimately demonstrate their deep understanding.

By using UbD, CTE educators can create programs that are not just a list of activities, but a clear, purposeful pathway toward professional mastery. To make the unit plan stronger, connecting a core academic standard not only adds rigor but also demonstrates the practical relevance of academic concepts to real-world CTE applications. For example, in a plumbing course, a math standard focused on problem-solving and proportional reasoning would be able to equip students with the skills to calculate water pressure, determine the appropriate size of a water heater, or troubleshoot drainage issues using mathematical formulas. After the appropriate standards are identified for the lesson plan, the teacher will need to define the objectives. The common acronym, SWBAT, which stands for "Students will be able to" provides language for the students and teacher to better understand the goal for the lesson. This can also lead to collaborative lessons with the core academic teachers. Partnering with a core academic class for a project or learning opportunity can help create deeper learning.

As discussed in Chapter 1, teenagers are at a pivotal point in their development and could have many different needs. Universal Design for Learning serves as a research-based framework to enable educators to address the variability of learners in a practical and systematic way (Meyer & Rose, 2024, p. 47). The central idea of Universal Design for Learning (UDL) is "predictable variability in learners" (Meyer & Rose, 2024, p. 44) which means, while there is "no average learner", the types of variability we see in the classroom are not random, and they are predictable patterns based on research. Students should not have to conform or be categorized to adapt themselves to the classroom; the learning environment should allow for individual variability (Meyer & Rose, 2024, p. 45). At the core, UDL is built on three principles that represent the learning network in our brains.

1. Affective Networks
   The "why" of learning is how we get engaged and motivated.
2. Recognition Networks
   Often referred to as the "what" of learning, this is how we gather and make sense of learning.
3. Strategic Networks
   In the "how" of learning, this network focuses on how we plan, execute, and monitor tasks.

Crucially, UDL is a proactive approach. Instead of retrofitting accommodations for individual students after a lesson is planned, UDL encourages educators to design flexibility and multiple pathways into the curriculum from the very beginning. This way, barriers are removed from the learning environment itself, rather than trying to "fix" the learner. Learners with agency are purposeful and reflective, authentic and resourceful, and strategic and action-oriented (Meyer & Rose, 2024, p. 51). CTE programs are inherently hands-on and skill-focused and designed to prepare students for real-world careers. This practical, applied nature makes a natural and powerful environment for implementing UDL principles. CTE thrives on performance tasks that directly provide multiple means of representations and multiple means of actions and expression. The goal of UDL is to develop "expert learners", learners who are purposeful and reflective, authentic and resourceful, and strategic and action-oriented (Meyer & Rose, 2024, p. 123). By intentionally designing for multiple means of engagement, representation, and action and expression, UDL empowers students to make choices, self-regulate, and pursue their learning in ways that are most effective for them, thus cultivating this crucial learner agency.

Since a core belief of UDL and best practices of teaching is meeting students where they are, differentiation helps accomplish this. Teachers need to be purposeful in their differentiation to meet the needs of the students. Modifying lessons and providing multiple learning opportunities is part of being a good teacher. To truly understand best practices in differentiation, it is important to develop a differentiation mindset. This includes seeing every learner with potential to succeed and recognizing, as the teacher you are responsible for removing barriers that exist to ensure equal access to learning (Tomlinson, 2014, p. 20). In creating a differentiated classroom, some best practices are as follows:

- ♦ Assessment is ongoing and responsive: Instruction is continuously informed by what teachers learn about their students' understanding and needs.
- ♦ Choice is center: Providing various opportunities to for students to make choices enhances engagement and relevance.
- ♦ Multiple materials are provided: Diverse resources cater to varied learning styles and accessibility needs.

It's common for differentiation to seem overwhelming if teachers think about giving each individual student a completely different assessment. However, true differentiation isn't individualized instruction; it is offering multiple avenues of learning (Tomlinson, 2014, p. 4). However, Carol Ann Tomlinson, a leading expert in differentiation, often breaks down differentiation for educators into four areas: content, process, and product (Tomlinson, 2014, p. 3). When teachers differentiate for content, the skill is taught to all students but the curriculum used might look different. For example, a teacher could use different texts based on student readiness levels or provide different text choices based on student interest (Tomlinson, 2014, p. 16). On the other hand, differentiating by process, students are still learning the same skill but have different pathways to learning it. An example in the classroom is learning stations to practice the skill. Lastly, the teacher can differentiate by product. Students will be assessed on the same skill but have a variety ways to demonstrate their knowledge (Tomlinson, 2014, p. 18). Teachers might use a learning menu of different project options or tiered products that students can pick from. Start small with thinking about differentiation. Consider lower prep ways you can offer options to students based on their readiness, interest, or learner profile. This includes varied choices in assignments and materials and different options for demonstrating knowledge. By incorporating UDL and differentiation, you are creating rigorous and personalized learning opportunities for your students to be successful.

Knowing strong lesson design is the foundation for then picking different instructional strategies. Primarily using the textbook as the only method of instruction is a common pitfall for teachers. While the textbook does offer information presented in sequential order, questions that prompt student thinking, and key information students need, it can also hinder student learning. In today's world, students can easily search and learn information on any subject within seconds. Textbook learning can be seen as a busy work task by students and lacks excitement and hands-on learning that students thrive on. While it is still critical for students to learn foundation knowledge and not rely on technology, teachers need to be creative in how they are engaging students in learning. Students need to be engaged, understand the why behind the lesson, and be participants in their learning. Building on the information in the textbook, there are a variety of ways for teachers to build their lessons using various instructional strategies and purposefully structure their lessons.

In the World Economic Forum, analytical thinking was the most sought-after skill by employers. Other skills employers ranked important in employees were resilience, flexibility, creative thinking, and a lifelong learner (World Economic Forum, 2025). Also outlined in the World Economic Forum's The Future of Jobs Reports 2025, technology changes, economic uncertainty, demographic shifts, and more will be significant in shaping the labor market by 2030. In the report that uses over 1,000 leading global employers, covering 14 million workers, certain trends emerge to help us think about the world of tomorrow. While the major theme focuses on the impact of broadening digital access and AI expected to transform business, there are other important findings. Frontline jobs like farmers, nurses, drivers, salespersons, and construction workers are expected to significantly grow. But what is really striking is that 39% of workers should expect their skills or be transformed or completely outdated (World Economic Forum, 2025).

## Class Structure

CTE classes, regardless of their length (40–160 minutes), require well-structured lessons for student success. Typically, time is divided between theory and practice. To ensure engagement during content/theory sessions, carefully constructing activities to foster learning and increase student motivation is critical. Many CTE teachers set schedules for theory work on certain days and shop/practicum work on the other days. One auto technology teacher I met did theory work every Monday. The rest of the week was dedicated to being in the shop. You have to find what works for your students. Depending on how often the CTE class runs and meets throughout the week, setting a set schedule allows students to better engage in class.

In the book, *Brain Rules* (2008), author John Medina suggests dividing presentations in 10 minute segments. As a guide, Medina suggests offering one large concept that can be explained in a minute. The brain processes meaning before details and like a hierarchy (Medina, 2008, p. 120). Introducing general concepts first helps students retain information and master content. It might be beneficial to try theory work in the first 20–30 minutes of class and then go into the shop.

The goal is to provide students with a mix of whole group instruction where new content is introduced, guided practice and collaborative work, and a space to individually practice the new content or skill. Students should be able to practice applying the new content or skill during the small group work. This time is vital for students to work together, ask questions, and take a risk.

The following are three different options for breaking up the class structure. The third option is based on if a class is much longer (in my district, we call this two blocks). What is missing from the class structure is time to change if the CTE program requires uniforms. Typically, students receive 5 minutes to change for physical education. Remember to set the expectations for the locker room, uniform, and changing with students.

| Structure 1–80 minutes | Structure 2–80 minutes | Structure 3–160 minutes |
| --- | --- | --- |
| Anticipatory set (10–15 min)<br>Whole-class discussion (10–20 min)<br>Small group work (20–30 min)<br>Whole-class share out (10–20 min)<br>Individual activity/exit ticket (20–30 min) | Anticipatory set (10 min)<br>Whole-class discussion (10–20 min)<br>Individual activity (10–20 min) | Anticipatory set (10 min)<br>Whole-class discussion (10–20 min)<br>Small group work (30 min)<br>Whole-class share out (20 min)<br>Individual activity/shop time (55 min)<br>Exit ticket (5 min) |

Structure provides students with clear pathways to learning. The routines set up in classrooms also allows students to take accountability for their learning by helping out with routines and procedures. Similar to elementary school, I assign my students jobs in the classroom. When I first introduced the idea of jobs and assigned students to jobs, my students rolled their eyes. You might be thinking the same thing as you read this. However, the jobs taught them habits in the classroom. The jobs I had in the classroom are the following: materials manager, playlist guru, property manager, and board eraser. The first few weeks, I had to remind students to complete their tasks. After a few rotations of jobs (because I wanted each student to get a turn), students were completing their jobs without a reminder and other students started to help out. The following school year, I forgot to assign jobs and my students automatically just started completing the tasks. Instilling these habits made a big difference in our classroom culture. Students were no longer blaming others for a mess but helping one another clean up. Consistency in the routine allows for predictability. Students will autonomously take on the classroom structure and own their learning.

## Instructional Strategies

Equipping yourself with different strategies for instruction helps make planning easier. All these instructional strategies can be changed to better fit the classroom content. When considering which instructional strategy to use, think about the following questions:

- ♦ What type of content am I teaching (factual, procedure, conceptual)?
- ♦ What level of engagement do I want to foster during this lesson?
- ♦ What resources and time available do I have?
- ♦ How will I know if students have successfully learned the content?

The first set of strategies is for strong opening and closing activities. Starting off the class with a specific routine helps students transition into the mindset of learning. Consequently, ending class with a specific routine helps students reflect on their learning, provides the teacher with insight, and allows for a clear end of the learning process.

## Anticipatory Set/Do Now

Starting the class with a purposeful activity allows students to shift their minds and better focus. Research supports the power of an anticipatory set. To be effective, a hook should trigger an emotion, be relevant, and be purposeful (Medina, 2008, p. 122). There are numerous options for anticipatory sets/do nows. These activities can also be used as exit tickets and customized to fit the class. Some teachers have a weekly schedule of do nows for the week. The following is a very basic example that a teacher can implement.

| Monday | Question of the day | **The teacher would have a thought-provoking question that connects to the lesson** |
|---|---|---|
| Tuesday | Vocabulary fun | Introducing a new vocabulary term and practice so students can grow their industry terminology |
| Wednesday | Case scenario | Have students look at case studies to understand the industry better |
| Thursday | What's wrong here | Find pictures that make students use critical thinking to understand what is wrong in the picture |

| Monday | Question of the day | The teacher would have a thought-provoking question that connects to the lesson |
|---|---|---|
| Friday | Reflection fun | Engage students in a protocol to reflect on their learning |

While the options are endless for bell-ringers, consider which ones are good for an extended period of time, easy to implement, and meaningful for the student. Keeping a weekly schedule does have its advantages, it is important to keep the schedule so students can benefit from consistency.

## Tool Tip 1: Community Builder

A community builder is a collaborative activity that serves as a way to promote community in the classroom and a type of do now. The purpose of community builders is to foster collaboration, problem-solving, and group work skills. When implemented, they strategically promote 21st-century skills. These are often misconceived as icebreakers. A community builder can be a fun activity that is led by the teacher or student. These activities focus on group work skills. Examples of community builders can be used in any program:

## This or That

As the teacher, prepare several different statements that students need to choose a side for. After saying the prompt, students will pick a side of the room. Ask students to defend their answer before moving on to the next prompt. This activity works well in the beginning of the year when getting to know students. Some basic prompts include the following:

Dunkin or Starbucks
Tea or Coffee
Winter or Summer
English or Math
Soda or Juice
Beach or Mountains
Marvel or DC

Extending on these basics, asking questions with two clear sides can also be asked for students to answer. Some examples of these include the following:

Would you rather be able to fly or be invisible?
Would you rather be able to travel to the past or travel to the future?
Walk through a rainforest or a desert?
Would you rather live on Mars or under the ocean?
Would you rather have a million dollars today or a penny that doubles every day for a month?

Another extension of this activity is relating it directly to content. This serves as a way to get students moving in the classroom and thinking about the topic of the day for class. For example, in carpentry class some this or that examples would be: measuring or cutting, working indoors or working outdoors, or using reclaimed wood or using new lumber. Students are able to form their own opinions and step away from technology. Another version of this is Four Corners. Create signs that say "Strongly Agree, Agree, Disagree, and Strongly Disagree" in four corners around the room. The teacher will read statements, and students will need to pick which corner of the room they agree with. The last version of this activity is Human Bar Graph/Human Scale. Similar to the original version, the teacher reads a statement and students form a human bar graph. The teacher can guide students to creating labels for the scale/graph.

## Picture Perfect

Giving directions and thinking outside the box are important skills for any trade. Identify several pictures, pieces of art, or tools and place them on a slideshow. There should be one picture for each slide. Have the students get into partners with one partner facing the board with the pictures projected and one partner that cannot see the board. The partner facing the board will give directions to the partner that cannot see the picture. The goal is to give directions without saying the picture. It forces the student to think carefully about word choice and how they explain something.

## Appointment Cards

As a discussion method, this strategy provides students with an opportunity to meet with three different people to discuss (Himmele & Himmele, 2017, p. 40). Another benefit is it gives students three different perspectives and encourages movement. Tell students to make three different appointments with students in the class. You can call appointments A, B, and C or assign artificial times like 8 a.m., 9 a.m., and 10 a.m. Students might be confused at first by the time but will understand once the activity starts.

At each appointment time, the teacher can have a question to discuss or topic. I often use a timer to keep students on topic and monitor the length of the activity. When planning this activity, I like to use three different questions and I have groups share out between the questions. The time limit allows students to focus on one topic and prevents students from going off topic during the discussion. This activity serves as a way to promote student critical thinking, encourage reflection on a topic, and active listening.

## What Doesn't Belong

To better build student argument skills, put pictures of similar items and have students argue which one doesn't belong. Students need to provide evidence and a justification for their thinking. This activity encouraged critical thinking and practice articulating their thoughts. Similar to other suggested strategies, you can make it related to your program or completely unrelated. An example is having different fast food restaurants, tools in a shop, or even different school supplies.

## Timed Challenges

Similar to the once popular show Minute to Win It, having students compete in time challenges focuses on bringing in play and fun into the classroom. There are many ways to do this but think about the purpose and skills you want students to engage in during the activity. You can even make timed challenges related to your program. Some examples are as follows:

- Paper Chain Challenge: Give students the same size construction paper and have them make the longest paper chain in a set amount of time. While this may seem simple, students need to think about measurements, use of materials, and divide up jobs.
- Comic Strip: Using comic strips in the classroom can promote critical thinking, collaboration, and engagement. You can find comic strips related to your CTE field or comic strips that have a specific message or humor. I cut the comic strip up and have the students work together to figure out the correct order. Afterward, I show students the completed comic. This activity pushes students to use their inference skills. We discuss the images and verbal clues in the comic. A possible extension is to have students create their own comic based on content in class.

Electrical One circuit building contest where students are given materials to build a proper circuit. Another idea is having students correctly strip wire with accuracy.

Cosmetology: Having students engage in a braiding, curling, or hairstyle contest fosters creativity and fun. Another idea is color matching. Students need to use dyes to match a color to test their color theory knowledge.

## Guess the Cost

Inferencing skills are important to teach life skills. A fun activity I play with my students is to guess the house price. I look through different housing listings to pick really exciting houses. I even find houses in different cities and countries. While real estate isn't related to our content, students have fun looking at different houses, working together, and they are engaging in critical thinking. It primes their mind to get into content for the day and in the zone of learning. You can modify this activity to any field. For example, you can have students guess the cost of a certain job someone needs done in their house or price of a hair stylist.

Community Builder Tip: During the first weeks of school, plan powerful community builders that energize students and focus on exploring content. After a few weeks, turn planning and facilitating community builders over to the students. Take time to discuss what makes an effective community builder, length of time, and different content students can use with their community builder. I usually have my students plan a community builder that lasts around 10 minutes. Students sign up for a specific date and content topic. This list is shared on our student learning platform for all to maintain.

## Tool Tip 2: Exit Ticket/Closing

While starting the class with a powerful anticipatory set is essential, the exit ticket is critical to wrap up learning and have students reflect on their learning. The exit ticket is commonly skipped over due to time constraints. However, exit tickets can be a good form of student evidence

## BrainSTORM or Brain Dump

A simple exit ticket that can be used at all points of a unit is the brainstorm. Give students a piece of paper that has an outline of a human head and have students write everything they remember from the lesson. Students can draw pictures, write words, or fill the paper with how they make sense of the content. It provides a space for students to make sense of the content and the teacher to see what students remember.

## 3–2–1 or Shapes

In reviewing materials, a 3–2–1 exit ticket will help students reflect on what they know and "stuck" with them during the lesson. Students record 3 things they learned, 2 questions they are wondering about, and 1 thing they are unsure about. Teachers can interchange any of the prompts. Another variation is using shapes, heart represents what did you love about the lesson, square represents what can you square aware/definitely know, and circle represents what do I need to circle back to.

## What Stuck With You? Or What's Next?

This exit ticket can be completed on a post. Students write down something that stuck with them at the end of class. Students can stick their sticky note to the door or whiteboard as they leave. This quick informal formative assessment can provide a lot of feedback. Ask students to reflect on how they plan to use what they learned and what they would do differently next time.

Reviewing exit tickets promptly allows teachers to gain actionable insights into student learning. These informal assessments serve as a valuable checkpoint, revealing areas of understanding and confusion that can inform future lesson planning and adjustments to instruction.

## Tool Tip 3: Instructional Strategies for Instruction

The thought of planning sounded overwhelming when I first started teaching. Even now, I sometimes get overly excited about a specific topic and want instruction to be perfect. The focus on instructional activities should be to allow students to practice the content, take risks and fail, learn from each other, and master content.

### Lectures and Direct Instruction

The desks in a row, student eyes glazed over. This might be a scene from a movie or some classrooms where lectures are primarily used. Lectures get a bad reputation for being boring. A lecture is when an educator stands in front of the class telling students about a specific idea, content, skill, or theory. Lectures and direct instruction are often used interchangeably but are different methods.

Direct instruction is when a teacher introduces a concept, models the concept, and guides the students in practicing this concept (Kilbane & Milman, 2014, p. 88). An example in cosmetology is the proper technique for a layered haircut. The teacher demonstrates each step on a mannequin or model and then lets students try by observing their work and providing feedback. Using the direct instruction model to teach procedural knowledge that is clearly defined, introduce new topics, reinforce skills, and teach techniques are benefits of this strategy (Kilbane & Milman, 2014, pp. 90–91).

## Gallery Walk

As discussed in Chapter 1, movement helps students learn. Gallery Walks serve as a way to get students moving and thinking. Create several different posters (on large poster paper or printed) and hang around the room. Students will go to each different poster and make comments, create questions, or share their thoughts. You can also have students write things down on a piece of paper as they go to each poster. Gallery Walks are typically silent, fostering focused reflection, and students can freely move from poster to poster or the teacher can time the students and have them go in a certain order. Another variation is to encourage students to use different colored markers at each station, allowing you to easily track contributions and identify patterns or have students write their thoughts on sticky notes, and then place them on the posters. This allows students to read other student's thoughts and add on to them. This activity is also beneficial for peer review. Have students post examples of their work, and have other students give feedback. By incorporating these strategies, you can transform a simple Gallery Walk into a dynamic and engaging learning experience that promotes critical thinking, collaboration, and movement.

Some ideas include showing pictures that students need to observe and make conclusions about, posting discussion questions or quotes for students to answer, displaying key vocabulary terms for students to define or use in sentences, or presenting real-world problem scenarios for students to brainstorm solutions. After the Gallery Walk, facilitate a class discussion to synthesize student contributions and address any lingering questions.

## Question Tail

To encourage movement and learning in the classroom, this strategy blends both together. When reviewing content, this strategy can provide a way to informally check for student learning. Create ten or more multiple choice questions on a slideshow. Each slide should be one question, and the answers should lead to another question. Print the slideshow, and hang the questions around the room. Students are able to start at any question. If students have the correct answer for all the questions, they will not repeat the questions. If students have a wrong answer, they will repeat a question. Students do not know which question is wrong, so they will need to trace their steps and carefully consider their answers. This strategy encourages critical thinking and self-reflection.

## Jigsaw and Group Work

Jigsaw instruction serves as an opportunity for students to own their learning and contribute to the classroom culture. In the Jigsaw strategy, students work in a group to teach their class about a topic. Each group in the classroom has a different topic. A teacher can give each group a topic, chapter, or section to be responsible for teaching to others and presenting the core information. As the teacher, creating expectations, guiding questions, and criteria for success contributes to meaningful student learning and collaboration. Students work together to become the experts and the best way to teach others. One example of how this is used in my classroom when teaching different theories of child development. I will have students in their groups pick a specific theory their group is interested in. Students will then become the expert of that theory and need to present it to the other student.

Students can contribute to a group slideshow where the information can be captured and shared with all students to review the content later. Students can also create posters that can be hung up around the room. This method allows students to own the learning, developing accountability and motivation. However, without clear expectations from the teacher, the jigsaw method can become artificial. One downfall that can happen is students regurgitating the information from a textbook without synthesizing that content. To overcome this, instruct students to create their own examples when thinking about complex concepts, develop their own scenarios or case studies, address common misconceptions, and facilitate a discussion. When students are done with their poster or presentation, students present. I will have students take notes, build on each one, and discuss similarities and differences to ensure they are actively listening.

Understanding the benefits of cooperative learning and how to create meaningful groups in the classroom can help students learn career-ready practices like working with others. When planning cooperative learning, one consideration is letting students pick groups or assigning groups. Being purposeful about assigning groups is essential and important to maximizing the benefits of it. Teachers may assign groups to minimize behavior problems, group students with similar abilities, or group students with different strengths to work together. Assigning groups mimics the real world where students do not get an opportunity to choose their coworkers. It allows students to begin to work with others who think differently. On the other hand, letting students choose their own groups allows students to feel empowered and brings joy to them. It can also be disruptive if students work with someone that causes disruptions. Having students learn social skills, problem-solving, and task management provides the opportunity for growth and students who can become adaptable. Being intentional about group work will contribute to overall classroom culture and community. There should be a balance of letting students choose groups and assigning groups. As the classroom teacher, consider the learning goal and length of the group work. Will the group work last several days, weeks, or one class? Is the group submitting a project together?

While there can be problems that arise during group work like behavior problems or lack of collaboration, there are ways to overcome and avoid these issues. To teach strong collaboration skills, providing students with group roles can prevent issues and show students how dynamic groups can function. Roles should be different from one another but also have a purpose. If group work is related to an ongoing and long-term project, having groups create a group contract allows students to have discussions about the "what ifs" and expectations before the project is started. Moreover, implementing clear expectations and a shared vision helps to eliminate the guesswork and allows students to focus on the task at hand. This could look like a checklist of things the group needs to accomplish. After introducing the project and all the components, allow students to create a group contract. The contract should include the following:

- Clear expectations for when working in the group.
- Assigned roles and responsibilities.
- Consequences for not completing tasks.

There are many different roles that can happen during group work. Consider the purpose of the work and what learning outcomes students should be focused on as a result of the group work. Depending on the purpose and focus, here are some traditional roles for groups that can be used when teaching content. Connecting soft skills to group roles allows a low risk way for students to practice their voice and agency.

1. Discussion-Based Role: In this role, students will be charged with facilitating discussion between the group members. The student will need to take ownership and extend beyond asking questions. This role will need to:
    - Prepare thought-provoking questions that encourage critical thinking and diverse perspectives.
    - Identify and highlight key points.
    - Maintain focus and direction.
    - Foster participation.

2. Recorder/Scribe: A student would be responsible for taking notes during the discussion or student meeting. This role will need to:
    - Take detailed notes.
    - Organize information.
    - Ensure accuracy.
    - Distribute notes.

3. Timekeeper: Encouraging students to be accountable for themselves and others is an essential skill. A group timekeeper allows the group to stay on task, manage their time, and work toward the goal. This role will need to:
    ♦ Establish time limits.
    ♦ Monitor time.
    ♦ Help with transitions.
    ♦ Keep the group on task.

4. Evaluator: Being able to evaluate, examine, and critique enables students to understand content better. This role includes:
    ♦ Providing constructive feedback.
    ♦ Examine content.
    ♦ Identify gaps and weaknesses.
    ♦ Encourage reflection.

When purposeful planning of group roles is considered, students are on task and have deeper learning. By assigning specific responsibility, we foster a sense of ownership and accountability, leading to increased engagement. Students are now active participants in their learning. This collaborative model also drives responsibility as students learn how to work effectively with others for a shared goal. Each student is aware of their part of the learning. To make group work even stronger, making CTE specific roles to reflect the real world promotes career readiness and a deeper understanding of industry expectations. Here is one example of CTE specific group roles:

Business Specific

1. Project Lead
2. Inventory Specialist
3. Quality Control
4. Market Researcher
5. Budget Analyst
6. Brand Manager
7. Communication Specialist

Plumbing Specific

1. Joining Specialist
2. Drain Specialist
3. Repair Specialist
4. Troubleshooting Officer
5. Code Compliance

Group work has numerous benefits when implemented with a strong plan. However, group work can lead to behavior problems. All the work may fall on one person's shoulders, groups missing deadlines because of a lack of communication, or interpersonal conflicts that arise from unclear expectations. As the leader, the CTE teacher can minimize these conflicts that can arise. While group roles and group contracts seek to address these problems, how can we resolve these conflicts as they happen?

Circulating during group work, observing groups, and providing timely interventions prevent minor issues from escalating. If the group work is going to be long-term, plan regular check-ins and reflection periods for groups. Create a log for students to complete to keep track of their work. As the teacher, keeping consistent with writing in a log, reflection, and check-in demonstrates the importance and builds good habits for students.

Beyond implementing numerous preventative strategies, we need to model conflict resolution and communication skills. Providing key instruction on how to handle disagreements on which direction to take the project and resources for students to turn to can equip students to handle disagreements and make them real for the "real" world. Setting clear boundaries for acceptable behavior and having an established process for unresolved conflicts give students a resource for handling disagreements. More importantly, give students the sentence that starts to have guided discussions around conflict resolution and strategies for overcoming the disagreement. As the teacher, modeling language and always focusing on the shared vision of the project make the conflict in group work less personal. When handling the conflict, be clear of the expectations of the group. Talk to students individually, and look at the work. Reviewing a log of everything the students have done and their specific role helps with having a hard conversation. By creating a culture of open communication and continuous improvement, we empower students to learn from their mistakes and strengthen their collaborative skills.

## Discussion Strategies

### Socratic Seminar
Providing a space for students to engage in a meaningful discussion allows students to learn key communication skills. Being able to disagree, question, and consider other perspectives is important for success in the real world. Socratic seminars have deep roots in educational history, dating back to Socrates. It provides a structured yet open-ended space for students to engage in a meaningful, in-depth discussion about a text, concept, or problem. This method goes beyond simple Q&A, encouraging students to actively listen, articulate their thoughts clearly, and build on each other's ideas.

In a CTE context, Socratic Seminars are invaluable for developing key communication and critical thinking skills that are highly sought after by employers. Being able to respectfully disagree, question assumptions, consider diverse perspectives, and articulate a well-reasoned argument is crucial for success in any real-world professional setting. Whether it's troubleshooting a design flaw with a team, debating the ethical implications of a new technology, or collaborating on a client project, the ability to engage in thoughtful dialogue is paramount.

There are many different ways CTE teachers can use this method in their classroom. This includes using case studies to discuss a real-world problem, debating interpretations on a complex based document, exploring ethical dilemmas, or analyzing industry trends. To prepare students to engage in a Socratic Seminar, start by selecting the text and have students annotate. Give students guidelines to interact with the text. This includes identifying key themes, highlighting important parts, creating questions, and making connections. Some teachers give questions to students to prepare for the discussion or let students create the discussion questions. Before the seminar, set some norms for discussions with students. These norms include the following: be prepared to listen actively, practice referencing the text, be open to changing your mind, and don't dominate. Students then sit in a circle and facilitate the discussion. Teachers take a back seat in the discussion. I often will ask for student volunteers to lead the discussion, take notes, and be a time keeper. This helps students take control of the discussion and their learning. Seminars can be a set amount of time or as long as students need to flesh out an idea. At the end of the discussion, have students individually reflect on their insights and performance.

**Hexagonal Thinking**
Hexagonal Thinking, a dynamic, hands-on discussion strategy (as detailed on Cult of Pedagogy), empowers students to forge meaningful connections between concepts (Betsy, 2020; Potash, 2020). By placing key terms, phrases, or figures on individual paper hexagons, educators create a tactile puzzle. Students then strategically arrange these hexagons, justifying the links they establish. This process encourages deep critical thinking and fosters a rich, interactive learning experience. In extending this activity, having students create their own hexagons or leaving 1–2 blank furthers student thinking. This activity can be used at the end of a unit to review content and better understand student thinking.

**TQE: Thoughts, Question, and Epiphanies**
In an effort to build more authentic discussions in my classroom, I came across the TQE strategy from an educator on Cult of Pedagogy's website (Unlimited Teacher, n.d.). Students are tasked with reading, listening, or watching something then formulating their own thoughts to contribute to discussion on their thoughts, questions, and epiphanies. I have students use this to question, evaluate, and engage in thinking. After students read, listen, or watch, I have them discuss what they can add to the class white board. Students send up one student to the board and write one to two things on each board. I pick one student

volunteer to lead a class discussion based on the contributions on the board. I found this method elicited student thinking, allowed me to assess what concepts students were struggling with, and revealed what information students were interested in.

## National School Reform Faculty

The National School Reform Faculty is a well-respected organization that developed powerful and adaptable protocols. These protocols are structured and intentional processes that help guide work to produce meaningful interactions, increase communication, and support learning. By providing a clear framework, the protocols guide participants through thought-provoking discussions, sharing of ideas, analyzing data, and critiquing content (National School Reform Faculty, 2025). Teachers can include these protocols to structure thinking and scaffold responsibility of learning to students. One strategy I find myself using time after time is the 4A protocol. This protocol is good when students read a chapter in the textbook, listen to a podcast, or just need a protocol to react to something. A simple piece of paper split into four sections that fosters students' thinking. Each section is a question: What do you agree with, what do you want to argue? What assumptions does the author hold? What parts of the text do you want to aspire to? (National School Reform Faculty, 2025). The simple organization of the paper allows students to consider different perspectives and engage with the text. What I also love is how easy it is to change/modify for my class. I sometimes change the questions or phrasing based on what I am teaching.

# Vocabulary

While some may think vocabulary instruction is just for English class or a mundane task, incorporating meaningful methods for vocabulary instruction promotes connections for students and builds important skills. In CTE, vocabulary is not just about words; it is the direct connection to the industry itself. Being exceptionally thoughtful and strategic about teaching industry-specific terms and jargon is paramount for student success, both in your program and in their future careers. Understanding this vocabulary isn't just about memorizing definitions; it's about comprehending the nuances, contexts, and specific applications of these terms in real-world scenarios. When students can confidently use and understand industry terminology, it immediately boosts their credibility. It signals to potential employers, mentors, and colleagues that they are serious about their chosen field and that they are "speaking the language" of the industry.

When deciding your vocabulary terms, think about the unit you are going to teach. What words are key for their understanding. Being able to explicitly teach these terms will also link to the bigger concepts. Introduce key terms *before* students encounter them in reading materials or complex demonstrations. Revisit them frequently in different contexts. Encourage students to use new terms in their daily conversations, lab reports, and project discussions. Model correct usage yourself. Here are some strategies to engage students in understanding vocabulary terms:

1. World Field Guide (O'Dell, 2021)

    A concept originally first published in the New York Times Learning Network by Rebekah O'Dell, this is a one page infographic that acts as a quick reference guide to the word chosen. Students are able to design a guide for that word. Students can use the New York Times Learning Network to find a word, explore its meaning in the context of the articles the word is used in, and delve into its broader implications. This promotes reading and contextual understanding.

    While some CTE programs will find using the New York Times Learning Network, teachers can modify it for their program. Students can create field guides for essential industry terms, jargon, acronyms, tools, and processes relevant to their program. When students begin to design the infographic, it forces students to move beyond rote memorization. They need to explain where and how the term is used, offer real-world connections, and create a visual representation.

Students can use a variety of digital tools like Canva, Google Slides, Adobe Express, or Microsoft to design their infographics. When students are complete, I always hang them around the room to serve as a word wall. The word wall serves as a resource students created together further demonstrating the importance of students taking the lead on their learning.

2. Bumper Words (Reading and Writing Haven, 2024)
For robust vocabulary understanding, utilize the bumper words. This activity encourages students to think critically about word meanings and identify subtle differences, and solidify their understanding of industry-specific terms. Here's how to implement it:
- Generate a unit vocabulary list.
- From the vocabulary list, create sets of four words. In each set, three words should share very similar meanings, contexts, and functions. One word should be a distinct outlet. The outlier can be a word from the list.
- Students identify the unique word in each group and determine why it doesn't fit.
    - Example Set 4 (Health Sciences): Diagnosis, Prognosis, Symptom, Prescription (Outlier: Prescription – a doctor's order for medication/treatment, others are related to medical assessment/outlook).
- Facilitate a discussion where students explain their reasoning, reinforcing word associations. This is where you can unpack nuances of the words to reinforce their definitions and connect to practical applications. Asking questions like "what would happen if you confused the words?'.
    - This activity encourages higher-order thinking, boosts confidence in the words, and promotes precision.

3. Word Wall
As students begin to learn industry terms, having a word wall in the classroom gives students repeated exposure to the word. The designated space displays the word and

definition. It serves as a passive and constant exposure to vocabulary. It also acts as a visual dictionary, so students can quickly reference the words. There are many different ways to use a word wall. Students can contribute words when they encounter them in their learning, a guest speaker, or project. Students can also group words on a word wall. For example, you can display pictures and have students group similar vocabulary terms next to the visual cue. Another modification is using questions to group the words or real-world scenarios.

## Authentic Learning Activities

I found myself becoming frustrated with students when they wouldn't care about the class assignment I created. They found no purpose or they felt like it was busy work. I was also spending time creating assignments that students seemingly didn't care about. I know some assignments were purposeful and important for the "fun stuff" we would eventually get to. However, students today need to see the why and understand the purpose behind something. I started to really reflect on what I was assigning. CTE naturally incorporates authentic learning. Students engaging with real-world tasks sets students apart when they enter the workforce. It is why so many students are drawn to CTE programs to begin with.

### Exploration of Industry Standards

Standards shouldn't be a secret from students as they are a roadmap to mastery. When students understand the purpose of the learning standards and the clear expectations tied to them, they transition from passive recipients of information to active, invested participants in their own educational journey. This transparency fosters a sense of ownership, self-direction, and accountability. Dissect a standard closely with students to help them identify the core action and the specific content. Once students understand the standard's intent, empower them to take the next step. They can create guiding questions, a metacognitive exercise that will help deepen their understanding. Additionally, students can help brainstorm and propose projects and learning activities. Students can even help in creating the projects. When students are able to see the standards as goals, rather than mysterious benchmarks, they can better track their progress. It also allows students to take control of their learning.

## Student Created Quizzes

Assessment is a key to understanding where students are in the learning process. While many students may complain about taking a quiz or test, flipping the scenario and having students create a quiz taps into student motivation. This approach not only transforms students from passive recipients to active creators but also fosters a deeper understanding of the subject matter.

First, I have students recall all the topics and content learned for the unit thus far. This serves an informal formative assessment, so I know what information and lessons really stuck with students. Then, provide students with instructions and parameters for the quiz. This could include a certain number of questions, answer to each question created, variety of questions (multiple choice, true/false, open-ended), and certain content that needs to be on the quiz. To ensure questions cover a range of higher-order thinking skills, I give students Bloom's taxonomy and Webb's Depth of Knowledge. This activity allows students to reflect on their own learning and identify areas where they need further clarification.

To extend this activity, students can peer review each quiz and create study guides. Students enjoy making hard questions their peers might get if the quiz is given. After students make the quiz, I review and will use their questions to create a quiz. When students take the quiz I made and see their questions, it boosts confidence and reinforces the learning process. By empowering students to create quizzes, we shift the focus from rote memorization to meaningful learning and active engagement.

## Newsletters for Alumni, Parents, or Community Members

Reading and writing are not just skills fostered and important in English class. Creating a newsletter that can be sent to different stakeholders enables students to understand the power of networking and communication. Using free platforms that have professional layouts like Canva helps create a professional newsletter that can be distributed. In high school, the communication between home and school becomes less. High school students don't always share everything that happens in the classroom. Creating a newsletter home bridges the gap between school and home.

First, share the goal of the newsletter with the students and brainstorm a list of sections for the newsletter. It can be a list of projects, guest speakers, field trips, or upcoming events in the program. Encouraging students to think about the audience is key. We have discussions around tone and important sections to include depending on the audience and purpose of the newsletter. Students choose which section they would like to write about and contribute to the newsletter. Additional sections can incorporate diverse media content like a video highlighting key skills, a short video clip of a guest speaker, or even a student spotlight. I have one student that volunteers to become our editor. This person is charged with picking out a template, editing all the sections, adding pictures, and making any final touches. To extend this activity, having students engage in peer review encourages shared accountability and constructive feedback. Lastly, share the newsletter with the identified stakeholder group! If the newsletter is going to parents, I will have students email their parents with the newsletter. It may seem elementary and students always groan when I first tell them but parents do appreciate it. Emailing the newsletter to alumni and the community can foster a sense of shared learning and ownership. Alumni and community members can make recommendations for new guest speakers, donations, or project ideas.

This authentic learning activity can be a 1–2-day class assignment or a long-term project. Students are learning the value of communication, understanding marketing and public relations, and how to engage with stakeholders. Even if students are going into a hands-on trade like carpentry or cosmetology, the importance of teaching students communication and marketing can make a difference in how successful a student is. To see how to build strong authentic learning projects, read Chapter 3.

## Technology and Platforms for CTE

The schedule of sending text messages truly changed my life. Being able to text someone and schedule it for a later date and time made me feel more accomplished and saved me from forgetting to tell people things. I like to call myself "techy" which really means I can complete basic tasks on a computer, phone, or other device. Thinking of how to include technology in the classroom is a challenge for many. However, as technology continues to change, my students teach me more and more about different functions of our technology like the schedule send feature for text messages.

Students today and in the future remain to be in an ever-changing environment inundated with the latest technology. Students seem to have shorter attention space and subconsciously reach for their phones. It also seems that students are constantly connected to a device in every single class. While recommending specific platforms might become outdated, teaching students to effectively leverage technology is enduring. Technology has the potential to "equal the playing field", make learning equitable, and have a profound impact on student learning. In CTE, this translates to developing strong problem-solving skills in digital environments. However, integrating technology poses challenges like ensuring its effectiveness and engaging students in a meaningful way. Similarly, students have different access to technology when at home and school. Students may have no technology access at home including Wi-Fi or have screen time limits set by their parents. The goal of technology in the classroom is to benefit student learning. Students don't need to be constantly connected to a device every single class. Using technology in the classroom should be meaningful, not an overuse of students sitting on a computer screen. Implement "tech-free" days where students can still work on similar skills but aren't attached to a screen, phone, or program.

There are hundreds of different platforms for CTE specific areas and many cost money. While schools may be willing to purchase different platforms for use, it is vital to carefully consider the platform and explore before making a purchase. Some platforms are used specifically for tracking hours when students attend their internship and can manage assignments like uploading internship check-ins, resumes, and other important information. There are platforms that can give real-life simulations for students to experience. Each platform has its advantages and disadvantages. Contacting companies for a free trial can help you decide if a platform is right for you and your school. It's okay to not know how to work every single piece of technology or know all the latest platforms. What is important is providing opportunities for students to engage with hands-on and applicable content. Technology is just one vehicle to deepen student learning.

In solving the challenge of overuse of technology, technology avoidance, or feeling confident in using technology, it is warranted to know the why behind using or choosing the technology (Sackstein & Laing, 2025, p. 77). Involving students in the process of choosing new technology applications or platforms can provide meaningful feedback and help in the decision-making process. As technology is constantly changing, teaching our students to constantly learn a new piece of technology is important. Encourage students to deconstruct unfamiliar software or apps, identify core functionalities, and apply them to real-world scenarios. Incorporate activities that promote collaborative troubleshooting, data analysis, and the ethical use of AI. Allowing students to document their trials, errors, and subsequent refinements reinforces important skills. This creates resilience and empowers them to confidently embrace emerging technologies, regardless of their prior experience. Invite students to share what they have found when exploring different pieces of technology.

When I wanted to introduce different child development theories, I had each group huddled around a computer chatting with a famous child psychologist. They were engaging with each other trying to think of the best questions to ask the AI bot disguised as a child psychologist. I used AI to have my students learn about the different theories from the actual source instead of the textbook. There are different websites that allow you to pick from a variety of historical figures to chat with. Some websites do require a subscription, but other AI tools don't. Always consult your district's guidelines before purchasing a tool or using it with students.

Each lesson might not go the way you want, and that's okay! It's in these moments of uncertainty that we learn the most. By embracing a mindset of continuous improvement, intentional design, and flexibility, we can find success. The goal isn't to be perfect, but to be purposeful, to plan with the student's needs in mind, to reflect on what works, and to remain open to adapting our approach. Ultimately, our greatest impact comes from a commitment to a collaborative process that allows us to meet every student where they are and prepare them for a world that is always changing.

 **Recommended Reading**

- *Embedded Formative Assessment: (Strategies for Classroom Assessment That Drives Student Engagement and Learning)* by Dylan William.
- *Instructional Strategies for Career & Technical Educators* by Michelle L. Conrad and Larae Watkins.
- *Next Level: Classroom Instruction for CTE Teachers* by Sandra Adams with Glenn Leininger.

 **Discussion Questions**

- Considering the emphasis on "bridging the gap of knowledge" before hands-on work, what is your *personal philosophy* on the balance between foundational content and

applied learning in CTE? How do you ensure students understand the "why" behind theoretical instruction?
- In what ways do you currently foster genuine student engagement, curiosity, and a sense of purpose in your lessons? Where do you see opportunities to deepen student participation and ownership of their learning?
- True learning is trial and error. How comfortable are you, personally, with allowing students to "fail forward" in your CTE classroom? What steps could you take to cultivate a learning environment where risk-taking and resilience are explicitly valued and taught?
- How can teachers intentionally build opportunities for failure, resilience, and iteration into their CTE curriculum and daily lessons, particularly when planning for hands-on activities?

## References

Advance CTE. (2025). *The National Career Clusters Framework*. Advance CTE. Retrieved May 23, 2025. https://careertech.org/career-clusters/

Betsy, P. (2020, September 11). Hexagonal Thinking: A Colorful Tool for Discussion. *Cult of Pedagogy*. Retrieved May 23, 2025. www.cultofpedagogy.com/hexagonal-thinking/

Hattie, J. (2023). *Visible Learning: The Sequel: A Synthesis of Over 2,100 Meta-Analyses Relating to Achievement*. Routledge.

Himmele, P., & Himmele, W. (2017). *Total Participation Techniques: Making Every Student an Active Learner*. ASCD.

JDEC. (n.d.). UbD in a Nutshell. https://www.jedc.org/stemak/sites/default/files/ubdnutshell.pdf.

Kilbane, C. R., & Milman, N. B. (2014). *Teaching Models: Designing Instruction for 21st Century Learners*. Pearson.

Medina, J. (2008). *Brain Rules: 12 Principles for Surviving and Thriving at Work, Home, and School*. Pear Press.

Meyer, A., & Rose, D. H. (2024). *Universal Design for Learning: Principles, Framework, and Practice* (D. T. Gordon, Ed.). CAST.

National School Reform Faculty. (2025). *What Are Protocols? Why Use Them?* NSRF. Retrieved July 25, 2025. https://nsrfharmony.org/whatareprotocols/

O'Dell, R. (2021, August 23). *Making Vocabulary Instruction Active With Language Field Guides (Published 2021)*. The New York Times. Retrieved July 31, 2025. www.nytimes.com/2021/08/23/learning/making-vocabulary-instruction-active-with-language-field-guides.html

Reading and Writing Haven. (2024, February 19). *5 Brain-Based Vocabulary Activities for the Secondary Classroom*. Reading and Writing Haven. Retrieved July 31, 2025. www.readingandwritinghaven.com/5-brain-based-vocabulary-activities-for-the-secondary-classroom

Sackstein, S., & Laing, A. (Eds.). (2025). *Solving School Challenges: The Everything Guide to Transformative Change* (1st ed.). Routledge.

Tomlinson, C. A. (2014). *The Differentiated Classroom: Responding to the Needs of All Learners*. ASCD.

Unlimited Teacher. (n.d.). *TQE: Thoughts, Questions, and Epiphanies*. Unlimited Teacher. Retrieved July 25, 2025. www.unlimitedteacher.com/tqe

World Economic Forum. (2025, January 7). *The Future of Jobs Report 2025 | World Economic Forum*. The Future of Jobs Report 2025 | World Economic Forum. Retrieved May 23, 2025. www.weforum.org/publications/the-future-of-jobs-report-2025/digest/

# 3

# Creating Authentic Learning Experiences

Before moving to teaching a CTE program, I taught English/Literature to high school students. I would assign a five paragraph essay after we read a class novel where many of my students would use SparkNotes or other sources to copy quotes and ideas from to write their essay. I would grade the essay and then the essays would sit in the memory of the computer, usually to never be opened again. I'll be honest, I felt like it was meaningless. I wanted my students to care deeply about their work and be proud of it. I wanted students to gain skills and demonstrate their knowledge. Instead, I was seeing how well students could repackage information we discussed in class or that they read online. It led to a deeper question, why did I have to assign the five paragraph essay? My students were never going to write that type of piece after high school. I also felt that my students were coming from amazing CTE courses excited about their work and I had to force commas and irrelevant information in their heads. I felt that I was wrong for feeling that way. This initial angst and feelings drove me to explore other project options and what best practice was in the field. Moreover, during the pandemic, I was pushed to reevaluate my assignments. What was their purpose? If students could just "Google it", what is the point?

While types of instruction like a traditional essay, presentation, quiz, test, or workshop can reinforce skills, concepts, and ideas, it doesn't always carry long-term learning or prepare students for the real world. What makes something an authentic learning experience? There are numerous benefits to having students engage in authentic learning projects like developing transferable skills like critical thinking, problem-solving, collaboration, and communication that are essential for success. The lessons I love the most are when I see students owning their learning, sharing it with others, and the excitement that comes over their face as they discuss their work. Creating that moment can take a lot of work. As I craved recreating that moment for my students more often, I found that regardless of the content area, there are certain criteria to creating these moments.

Authentic learning projects have three main characteristics: connect to the real world, integrate skills, and a real audience. When students are able to engage in authentic learning tasks, they have to define the tasks for themselves, create and produce a polished product, and reflect on their work (Stanley, 2018, p. 5). Students should engage in similar practices as industry professionals. For example, for culinary arts CTE students, instead of only practicing cooking techniques in a classroom kitchen, culinary arts students could plan, prepare, and serve meals in a student-run restaurant open to the public. Students would demonstrate their transferable skills learned and gain industry-level experience. At the core of an authentic learning project is student choice, accountability, and reflection. Student choice is important to boost student engagement and motivation but also fosters a sense of independence and confidence. Providing students with agency over their learning is a core UDL principle, directly linking to research on the brain and learning.

When creating authentic learning projects, start with the standards and then consider the real-world context and application by identifying relevant problems, issues, or skills that students will need to succeed in their career field. Clearly define the authentic "end product" students will create or the real-world "challenge" they will solve. This could be designing a component, troubleshooting a system, developing a business plan, or performing a specific industry task. I've personally experienced the pitfall of crafting projects that, while "amazing" and enjoyable, failed to connect meaningfully to core learning standards and, as a result, served little ultimate educational purpose. One example of this is when students created their dream classroom. It was fun to have students visualize their dream classroom but solely focused on the aesthetic instead of classroom management principles. Avoiding this common pitfall can help shape student learning. Next, determine what content, skills, and ideas will need to be addressed. At this stage, consider the technical terms, vocabulary, and content students truly need to understand to engage in an authentic learning project. Use the language in the standard to guide the planning for this. Also, consider prior knowledge of learning. During this process, you can begin to brainstorm different learning activities. Learning activities are the class lessons or activities that help students master skills. Incorporate time for structured reflection. Students should analyze their process, what they learned, challenges they overcame, and how their project connects to real-world career competencies. This metacognitive practice solidifies learning and highlights growth.

Consider what guest speakers could enhance the project and learning or where students can showcase their work. After, begin the planning for the project. A best practice is to start with the end of the project in mind. Pick a date for the final project and work backward, what content needs to be taught, how many different workshop days do students need, and what are the checkpoints for the project.

While authentic learning experiences, in my opinion, is an umbrella term, there are similar types of learning that promote real-world experiences, ignite student curiosity, and foster important skills for students. Problem-based learning, project-based, and challenge-based learning are a few different strategies for implementing real-world learning in the classroom.

When thinking of authentic learning, be careful to fall into the trap of just creating simulations, but true authentic learning involves genuine tasks that mirror professional practice. Make a list of industry related projects that students would engage in once they enter the industry. This list can be made through Advisory Council, networking with industry professionals, your own knowledge in the field, and staying current with research.

## Project-Based Learning

Project-based learning (PBL) is a method where students gain knowledge and skills by working on an authentic, engaging, and complex problem (PBL Works, n.d.-a). There are essential characteristics of PBL like critical thinking, problem-solving, collaboration, high-quality work, and creativity. Buck Institute for Education has a strong framework to follow. It includes seven essential project design elements which are authenticity, student voice and choice, sustained inquiry, challenging problem, public product, critique and revision, and reflection (PBL Works, n.d.-b).

Four different research studies show that using rigorous project-based learning has positive student outcomes (Lucas Education Research, n.d.). Students performed significantly higher on all measures of student assessments like AP tests, state tests, and reading assessments. More significant is that the projects were central to the curriculum, and students were interacting with the project and high-quality resources each day. This is a common misconception when implementing project-based learning. So, what term to use? Authentic learning, PBL, project? PBL projects have a specific framework, introduce a problem, and have students investigate the problem to create solutions. This framework is easy to implement, providing clear steps and highly effective for critical thinking. Authentic learning refers to an approach, a philosophy that does include PBL. No matter what term you use, understanding how to create a meaningful project is fundamental.

Here is an example of a healthcare project under each category.

| Project | Project-based learning project | Authentic project |
|---|---|---|
| Create a presentation detailing the impacts of diabetes on a patient long term | Design an interactive patient education tool for newly diagnosed diabetes patients, addressing misconceptions and promoting adherence to treatment plans | Participate in a simulated emergency room scenario with defined roles |

What are the core elements of an authentic learning project?

- Pick learning standards that you want to assess (this could even be your unit standards)
- Design project that allows for sustained inquiry
- Create a driving question that frames the project and promotes student thinking
- Provide specific instruction to allow for meaningful learning
- Collaboration, revision, student voice, and student choice
- Share Out to a wider audience
- Reflection

This checklist will allow for you to think specifically about the details. As teachers, we see our vision but students may see a different vision or not understand ours yet. Being aware that we might have missed thinking of an important aspect is okay.

One example of this in action is in a welding class.

Project: Create a series of functional or decorative metal products from recycled or repurposed materials.

Driving Question: How can we transform discarded metal materials into valuable and desirable products through the art of welding, promoting sustainability?

Student Project: One example is a garden stand/metal planter. Using old metal buckets, cut water heater tanks, and old auto rims, the student was able to use materials to create a multi-level planter for someone to use.

Skills Learned: The student really had to consider how to combine materials and also consider how to make it aesthetic for a person. Further, the student had to consider how to ensure proper drainage and weather resistance.

Interdisciplinary projects between academic or other CTE programs provide an opportunity for students to transfer their learning and strengthen their ability to apply knowledge and skills across different contexts, preparing them for further success. It also further demonstrates how deep rooted some academic subjects are within CTE. Students are able to better understand some concepts because in the real-world, there are no clear boundaries. One example of an authentic project was between a biotechnology and English classes to learn about bioethics. In this project, the biotechnology students taught an introductory lesson on bioethics to the English class as they read *Frankenstein*. After the students reviewed bioethics and practiced with case studies, students from biotechnology and English debated on current issues in bioethics.

There can be possible challenges when creating authentic learning projects. The main challenges are time constraints and resources. Start small and think about one change to make to a project to make it authentic. Each project doesn't need to be a grand scale event with numerous outside guests. The most important thing is to remember what students are learning and the process. It can be easy to get lost in the outcome. When planning a project, always start with the end date and work backward. Adding 2–3 days of "wiggle room" allows for any last minute schedule changes or if students need help with a certain topic.

Some authentic projects require materials, training, and resources that need to be purchased. There are many ways to gain resources for projects. Applying for outside grants is one way to secure supplies, materials, or support for students to complete projects. However, the most successful ways to gain resources is through networking with other teachers, asking advisory councils, and proper budgeting. Communicating needs early with the direct supervisor can help in gaining the resources necessary. Seeking grants and asking companies to donate materials, resources, or professionals build community partnerships and strengthen the connections with the companies.

Here are some types of authentic learning projects to incorporate in any classroom that can work in CTE program:

Video Essay
    While traditional essays have a specific purpose, a video essay adds a different layer of skill for students. A video essay can be focused on analyzing a problem presented

and students giving their opinion/solution. Students can also have students film a How to Video. Video essays encourage students to practice their public speaking, but they also develop a range of other crucial skills, including visual communication, digital literacy, and creative storytelling. Students need to properly plan their video essay before filming which taps into skills they use in English class. One example for an auto class is "Create a detailed, step-by-step 'how to' video demonstrating a specific automotive maintenance task that can be safely performed by a beginner". The prompt and video assess their knowledge on the steps for basics. It also can demonstrate how students would speak to customers that lack knowledge about their cars. A video essay integrates technology skills, so students can practice strategic planning, using different equipment, and editing skills.

Podcasts

With millions of listeners and a myriad of ways to listen, podcasts are consumable, accessible, and authentic projects for students. Students are able to create their own topic and episode based on their interest. Podcasts are accessible for students to create if they have access to a computer or cell phone. At the start of the project, we spend time listening to podcasts that interest us or relate to the content we are studying. Students evaluate how well the podcast did in engaging the audience, how the speakers presented evidence and stories, and how sound was used.

Students then brainstorm an idea for their own podcast. I give them prompts and parameters to think about as they create their own podcast. The following is a prompt I give my grade nine students when we explore the history of education:

Prompt: Education doesn't exist in a vacuum. It's shaped by the shifts, cultural events, and technological advancements that define our society. But how deeply do these external forces ripple through the walls of classrooms and impact the way we learn and teach?

*Your task is to create one episode (10–12 minutes long) around your topic that explores the enduring impact.* Your podcast should be well-researched, timely, and reflective of the topic.

I even provide sample topics that students can use if they have trouble getting started. Two examples are:

- The Origins: Trace the historical roots of [Topic] and its initial encounter with the realm of education. How did it first challenge or inform teaching practices?
- Echoes in the Curriculum: Explore how different educational disciplines have grappled with and incorporated your topic. How has it shifted content, approaches, and even the definition of "literacy"?

Podcasts allow for creativity, develops literacy skills, boosts engagement, and fosters critical thinking. With a podcast, students have to create an outline. Students might feel like they are a "safer" assignment because they are verbally communicating their work. Writing can be hard and a mental block for students. Podcasting builds confidence that can transfer into other areas like presenting. More importantly, amplify student voice and ownership.

Ideas for other programs are as follows:

- Carpentry students can create a podcast documenting their journey on a specific build. They can also create a podcast on a specific tool where they can go over the history, essential safety tips, common mistakes made when using the tool, and even a myth vs fact segment.
- Welding students can interview industry professionals and create a podcast sharing stories from the trade.
- Cosmetology students can dive into issues like skin, nails, and hair. Further, they can look at different salons, beauty stores, and famous stylists and evaluate them.

## Industry Scenarios and Projects

Consider creating industry related scenarios and projects in the classroom. These are the projects that reflect the industry. For example, a design program has a form for teachers, students, clubs, and sports to be completed when they need artwork, graphic designs, or posters. When someone completes the form, it is emailed to the teacher that then assigns the project to a student. The student is tasked with communicating with the client and completing multiple drafts until the project is complete. An auto class might work on staff members' or community members' cars. These might sound like large projects that are significant undertakings. Healthcare students might run a 1-day clinic to community members offering free fitness plans for attendees or educational awareness campaigns. To begin, start small. A smaller project could be designing brochures, a website, or t-shirts for a small business.

Whatever size project you decide to take on, the values remain the same. Think about developing a strong workflow and think about the details. Do you need an intake form to gather details from the client? How will you ensure quality work to the client from each student? Be sure to allow time for multiple drafts, feedback, review, and final delivery. You want the project to teach students the industry but also the soft skills: communication, confidence, and professionalism.

### Museums and Exhibition

Student displays of work showcase mastery of information and careful planning. Museum projects are a fun way for students to synthesize information and allow students creativity. Students are typically tasked with designing an exhibit space/proposing a new display for a museum. As the teacher, you can make it specific to your CTE program, so find a museum where students can look at their current exhibits and explore the mission of the museum. Students can create formal proposals that are written that include budget, layout, research, and how it would link to the museum's vision. Students can also create a 3D model of the exhibit to display.

**Infographic and One Pagers**

Being concise and organizing information is an important skill for students to learn. Students have mastered the art of the fluff. They can write the same thing over and over. Infographics are a visual display of information. Students need to think carefully about how to present information, what words they need to specifically choose, and what images help enhance the content. Infographics also teach students how to use different types of data for visualization like using graphs, pie charts, and line graphs. It also forces students to think about when to use different types of data. Students also need to consider the flow of data and how to have a clear narrative flow.

One pagers are a creative way for students to think strategically about information. Think about each section as a way for students to think deeper about a specific topic. For example, sections can be the most challenging concept, connection to the real world, if I were the expert, key takeaway, favorite tool, and many more. The goal is to synthesize the information and avoid superficial summaries. Students can create visual metaphors to demonstrate their understanding.

With both of these options, students need to consider purpose and audience. It helps students make deliberate decisions rather than fill space. To help your students, have them think "what specific action or understanding do you want the audience to gain?". This can help drive the information they add to the visual organizer. To create a professional infographic or one pager, I have students use Canva. There are other tools out there, but Canva is ready to use templates and offer free professional accounts to teachers.

## Presentations

Presentations are a tried and true method to have students demonstrate and master public speaking skills. However, when students present to each other, some students zone out during presentations or the students presenting find it meaningless. Having students present to other stakeholders like parents, other educators, or community members raises the importance and purpose for the presentation. Presentations can look similar to a traditional slideshow or something different. One option for presentations is an exhibition/science fair model. Students can have a station around the classroom that guests visit and rotate through. This takes the pressure off a large presentation but allows students to have multiple opportunities to present and have discussions around their work.

While there are many benefits to having students present, it can be time consuming for students to present. Consider how long presentations should be when assigning a presentation to a student. If your class has 20 students in it and each student presents for 5 minutes, that equals to 100 minutes of presentations. Have students sign up for a presentation time slot prior to the deadline. Break up the presentations into 2 or 3 days depending on the number of students and time of presentation.

Prior to students presenting, be sure to comb through the projects. It may seem excessive, but it avoids a few different issues. First, students may put something inappropriate or hurtful in their presentation. Taking a proactive approach to vetting the presentations prior to sharing with other students and adults saves awkward conversations later. You also don't want anyone in your audience uncomfortable. Second, students may fail to submit or fully develop their presentation. Instead of lettering students failing, pull them from the presentation list ahead of time. It avoids embarrassing the student and demonstrates professionalism.

Questions to Consider:

- How could the learning tasks connect to the real world?
- How could students have more voice, choice, or ownership?
- How could collaboration be more meaningful?
- What would a "product" or "outcome" look like that goes beyond a grade?
- How could reflection be integrated?

**Community Partnerships**
Authentic projects thrive when students can showcase their work and connect with the community. Despite the significant undertaking of planning and hosting a community event, the resulting stakeholder engagement, sense of belonging, and shared learning experiences offer profound benefits.

Community and school-wide events provide the ideal opportunity for prospective students to interact with students and staff from the school and promote a sense of belonging. Planning and hosting events are a lot of work, but when sharing the leadership with others, the stress is minimal. Involving students in the planning and hosting process also relieves stress and teaches valuable lessons. Brainstorm different ideas with the students on events. A CTE school is the prime location to host a career fair for high school students. Invite local businesses and organizations to host tables. Include a variety of different workers to showcase the multitude of careers available. Use social media to post the event and share! Including the community opens opportunities for the community members to thrive and build trust in the school as well. Similarly, hosting a career pathways night where each career program can host a table with an interactive element for middle school students can help encourage students to explore various career pathways and also strong marketing for the school. Students from each program can plan the table. Students would then be tasked with hosting the table the day of the event. This affords them an opportunity to demonstrate their skillset, teach others, and inspire others.

Demonstrating their understanding of educational needs, future teachers organized events at local elementary schools. Recognizing the importance of parent engagement and robust teacher professional learning during their math and reading pedagogy studies, they conceived of family nights to build parental confidence in supporting student learning. After collaborating with the principal to determine key topics, the student teachers translated their theoretical knowledge into practical application by designing interactive stations aligned with state learning standards for students and their families. Integrating community partnerships to support students in the creation of learning experiences extends the benefits beyond events, offering practical application and deeper engagement.

Another example of a community partnership is various CTE programs working together to host an event. In a recent event held, students from three different programs worked together with local organizations to hold a Teddy Bear Clinic. Teddy Bear Clinic aims to bridge a gap between children being scared of first responders and hospitals. They are often hosted by hospitals and police officers. For this event, students from an education, health care, and law program created stations to host and communicated with local first responders and vendors to create a family event. This event had over 150 local children attend and 5 local first responder agencies. This event was able to expose younger children to first responders which desensitizes children to the scariness of first responders. More importantly, it provides an opportunity for children to learn what to do in case of emergencies and proper safety protocols. What is the secret of planning such a large scale event? First, communicate with all professionals on the purpose and roles of each person. Being clear about expectations, roles, and the why allows each person to contribute to the large scale event. Second, careful planning and involving student voices are important. Let students plan and involve them in the preparation. After seeing the event, many local agencies wanted to contribute financially for the next year.

In creating meaningful community partnerships, start small. Contact local organizations that could benefit from a partnership. One example of a smaller yet impactful community partnership is a design program painting the windows of the town's downtown shopping area for an event. Each year, the town hosts an event to raise awareness for breast cancer awareness. To contribute to the event and raise awareness, the design program walks to the downtown area and paints windows for the town on the small businesses. Another example of a smaller partnership is a cosmetology program going to a nursing home to provide free hair and nail services to the residents once a month throughout the year.

My supervisor forwarded me a global writing contest for students to advocate for a local change. The students were tasked with identifying an issue in their local communities, arguing why the issue was important, and recommending solutions to send it to local elected officials. I loved every aspect of the project. It provided students with the opportunity to pick a local issue that was important for them while teaching them about how to make change in the community and the power of their voice. We spent weeks researching, drafting, and revising before sending our letters to the contest and emailing the local elected officials.

A few days after sending our emails, I received an email from my superintendent asking for a meeting as soon as I was free. I immediately panicked thinking how I was in trouble. The minutes and hours until my free prep took years off my life. As the bell finally rang, I sprinted to his office to await my fate. My superintendent asked me a few questions about the letter project I did with my students and my process. He soon revealed he received a frantic phone call from a local official thinking our school has a serious problem. I quickly realized my mistake. I failed to communicate the project and now wasted the time of various leaders in my community. My superintendent asked that next year, I inform him when the project is happening. While he was supportive of the project, he needed communication, so he could speak to various leaders on the project in case they called. Leaving that meeting, I felt better but still like I had made a huge mistake. I even thought about not doing the project in the future the following year. After talking to my supervisor, she encouraged me to stick with it. This was a tiny lesson, and the student outcomes were worth much more than beating myself up over a small mistake.

Communication is essential when implementing an authentic learning project or task. First, communicating directly with your supervisor avoids getting called into an office to be scolded. It can also lead to stronger support. Think about how much parent communication you need to have for the project.

## Student Competitions and Clubs

There are numerous organizations that offer contests for students to enter. There are a number of Career and Technical Student Organizations (CTSO) that offer competitions and contests for students to compete in. Your school may already have an established CTSO, or you can start one at your school. Each CTSO aims to mirror industry, providing students with applied learning and real-world application but also leadership and personal development (CTSO, 2024). Students can compete locally and move through to the national competitions. Students can also apply to hold leadership positions at the local, state, and national levels. Understanding the different CTSOs can be helpful in planning competitions. The following are established and nationally recognized CTSOs: DECA, Business Professionals of America, Future Business Leaders of America, Family, Career and Community Leaders of America, HOSA, SkillsUSA, Technology Student Association (CTSO, 2024). From the earlier list, some CTSOs are for specific industries like DECA or HOSA. DECA focuses on preparing students for careers in marketing, finance, hospitality, and management (DECA, n.d.). HOSA is specifically for students interested in healthcare. One of the largest CTSOs is SkillsUSA. Its mission is to empower students to become skilled professionals, career-ready leaders, and responsible community members. The SkillsUSA framework blends personal skills, workplace skills, and technical skills to best support students. The organization has been supporting CTE since 1965 when it was known as the Vocational Industrial Clubs of America. In 2004, the organization officially changed its name to SkillsUSA and now has over 400,000 student and teacher members (SkillsUSA, n.d.). If your school is part of SkillsUSA, there will be a dedicated chapter advisor. Schedule a time to meet with them to better understand how you can support your students competing at SkillsUSA.

Using the CTSO's resources in planning lessons and preparing for competition takes the burden off lesson planning but also ensures high-quality instruction. Students have the opportunity to meet students that are also studying similar programs, gain leadership skills, and demonstrate their knowledge. Competing in the competitions provide students the opportunity to showcase their skills but also connect with other students in similar programs.

The New York Times Learning Network is another place to find contests and resources that CTE students can use. Using timely and relevant articles can help students connect to the world around them and be part of a larger conversation. Each year, the NYT Learning Network offers a calendar with different competitions. While some contests may seem like it should only be used in English class, it is important to show students how integral writing and speaking skills are in the industry. Some example contests are as follows:

- Multimedia Contest: This contest asks students to make something (poem, narrative, podcast, photograph, or more) in response to a variety of questions.
- How To: This is informational writing contest that challenges students to write a short description on how to do something. This contest is a great way to measure how students have mastered a skill. In writing this piece, students need to interview an expert and quote them in their How To.
- Open Letters: Opinion writing contest focuses on students forming opinions surrounding an issue. We need to teach our students to be fierce advocates for what they are passionate about. This contest affords the opportunity for students to shape and share their own opinions.
- Podcast Contest: This contest is a unique opportunity for students to master their speaking skills in creating podcasts. The podcast can be focused on anything. Students can think about a topic within their CTE field to speak about and make relevant for listeners.
- Vocab Video Contest: This contest compels students to create a 15 second video defining and explaining a specific word.
- Word Field Guide: This guide also focuses on creating a visual representation of a specific word.
- One Pager: This is a creative way for students to synthesize information in response to a specific *New York Times* article.

Some of the contests are better for some career programs than others. However, by students submitting their work to a contest, it enhances their motivation to do well. It makes the learning "real". Be open to trying a contest that may seem untraditional for your program.

There are many companies and organizations that provide contests each year. The list is ongoing and ever-changing. Be sure to do your research when deciding if you should have your students enter. Never force a student to submit their work to a contest if they are uncomfortable. Communicate with your supervisor that you are submitting student work. You might need to also get parent permission before submitting. Here are some questions to consider as you explore the contest:

- What is the mission and vision of the company and organization? Do they have any potential conflicts or biases?
  - What is the company or organization reputation? Are they well-respected?
- How does this contest align with the standards and skills I am teaching?
- What are the potential drawbacks from competing in this contest?
- What happens to submitted student work? Does the company/organization retain the rights?

## Careful Planning Considerations

Authentic learning projects can take a significant amount of planning and involve numerous moving parts. Start small and build up. You don't need to tackle a massive project immediately. Think about one project you love and start by revising it. Careful planning and thinking about the small details are important. What is one way you can change the audience of a project? How can you incorporate student choice? This might look like students picking what the project product is or the driving question.

Establishing a timeline for different benchmarks is the first step in careful planning. It might be old school, but I print out calendars and put non-negotiable dates like end of the marking period, any days off from school, or other important dates in pen.

I pick the date I need the project to be completed and put it in pencil. Being aware of important dates will help better plan your due date. Dates like midterms/finals, end of marking period, long breaks, and major school events impact students. I try to avoid having a major project due at the same time as the end of the marking period. Students are usually stressed and have multiple projects. Like all projects, build in extra time in case things take longer. What should students know and be able to *do* by the end? What will the final authentic assessment look like? Once these are clear, you can work backward to map out the necessary skills, knowledge, and instructional activities.

Consider resources and materials needed. Will you have all supplies for students to complete this project? What potential issues can arise? You can even use AI as a thought partner to think of creative ways to overcome hurdles and anticipate challenges with the project.

## Strategies to Scaffold Authentic Assessments

Scaffolding is like building a temporary support structure around a learning task. It helps students reach a higher level of understanding or skill than they could on their own, and then, as they become more capable, those supports are gradually removed. This approach is absolutely vital in CTE, where projects are often complex and require mastery of many new skills simultaneously. Authentic learning projects should be integrated into the curriculum. Thus, each lesson every day should be part of the authentic learning project. Embrace failure of learning in the classroom. Creating a safe environment where students can earn from mistakes and troubleshoot their project mirrors the industry and creates deeper learning. Here are some strategies to help scaffold authentic learning projects:

### Project Wall

Bucks Institute for Education recommends a project wall to have students visualize key information as it unfolds (PBLWorks, n.d.). The wall includes images that represent different parts of the project, but more importantly the wall includes important information and visual cues. This includes learning outcomes, the driving question of the project, common questions, project calendar, key dates, and deliverables. The wall can even include key vocabulary, rubric, sample work, and tips for the students. It serves as a central reminder how significant the project is.

| Planning | Research | Production phase | Review and revision |
|---|---|---|---|
| Project proposals Mind maps Checklist for deliverables Project timelines | Curated research list Guided note-taking Mini-lessons | Mini-lessons Peer mentoring Checkpoints | Rubric walk-through Peer feedback Revision checklists Presentation practice |

### Skill Pre-Teaching and Mini-Lessons

Assuming students already possess these skills, or expecting them to acquire them "on the fly" while grappling with project concepts often leads to frustration, errors, and a diminished quality of work. Instead, being purposeful in your lesson planning means breaking down the project into its foundational technical components. By mastering smaller, manageable skills in a low-stakes environment, students develop the confidence necessary to tackle the full project. They know they have the foundational abilities needed. For example, in cosmetology, instead of moving directly to haircuts, the first lesson would be learning how to properly section the mannequin's head.

### Celebrating Success

Beyond grading students and providing the authentic learning experience, it is important to celebrate student success and highlight the accomplishments. When students win a contest, receive recognition from a company, or accomplish a large goal, think of ways to celebrate their success. These moments show students how important their hard work is and the results of their labor. There are many ways to celebrate students that are at no cost to the teacher.

School Website and Social Media: Showing the accomplishments of students on the school website celebrates their accomplishments and highlights the school. You can create a post that the school can use on their various social media pages or send the information to the designated person for social media at your school. If you are unsure about who that person is, contact your supervisor.

School Board Meetings: Talk to your direct supervisor about recognizing students at a Board of Education meeting. The school may have a specific board meeting for awards each year. At the board meeting, the superintendent can present a certificate and highlight the student. After, a reception can be held with coffee and desserts.

Local Media Coverage: Submitting good news to the local news and newspapers helps spread the word about student accomplishments. Before submitting any student to the local news, you should discuss with your supervisor and the student's parents.

Pep Rally/School Assemblies: One of the best ways to recognize students is in front of their peers. During a school-wide assembly, think about ways to make it fun and inclusive for all students.

Mimic Industry Ceremonies: Just as a nursing pinning ceremony marks the transition from student to professional, a CTE pinning ceremony signifies a student's readiness to move from high school-level training to either higher education in their field or direct entry into the workforce. It provides a formal acknowledgment of their acquired skills and dedication. For students who have dedicated years to a CTE program, this ceremony offers unique recognition that might not be as prominent in a general high school graduation. It celebrates their specialized achievements and rigorous hands-on training. Think about if your industry has a unique ceremony similar to nurses that you can host for your students.

When seniors are graduating, you can also consider giving students pins or cords to wear at graduation.

## Teacher Spotlight

Troy Reichert is not a stranger to students working on large community projects that make a difference for all stakeholders involved. Troy Reichert's educational philosophy is a testament to the power of authentic, project-based learning. His core teaching model redefines the classroom, transforming it into a dynamic workshop where students are immediately immersed in hands-on projects that benefit both their learning and the wider community. Reichert's students are currently working on remodeling the Veterans of Foreign Wars in the local area. He likes to teach in the classroom as little as possible. From the moment students step into his shop, Reichert prioritizes putting tools in their hands and explaining their use, fostering an immediate, authentic connection to the work. He stopped using the textbook over 20 years ago. When we discussed how CTE teachers can move beyond "old school" teaching methods while ensuring students acquire the necessary knowledge to work on large jobs, he focused on how he embraces the current ways students consume information. He cites YouTube as one source to teach students how to work with tools and blends important content knowledge with key skills students need. Reichert recognizes that textbooks quickly become outdated and students enrolled in his CTE program want to get their hands moving. Further, he recommends actively bringing industry professionals and leaders into the classroom for students to extend their content knowledge. Hearing the same information from someone working in the field can be significantly more beneficial and authentic for students than hearing it solely from their teacher. It can serve to confirm classroom teachings and bridge the gap between theory and real-world application.

Moreover, allowing students to become leaders in the classroom helps build capacity. Seniors can serve as foreman on projects as they keep the project running and oversee the day to day. Freshmen serve as an apprentice and build skills. He also credits the success to exposing students to CTE in middle school. During 7th grade, students learn the basics of tools and work on simple projects. As students move on to 8th grade, they go through a rotation of different trades like welding, plumbing, electrical, and more to get a sample of different pathways. Students can have a comprehensive understanding of each pathway before choosing for their high school career.

Sometimes, he admits that CTE teachers are their own worst enemies. We worry about taking the first steps, making a phone call to a stranger or being told no. Reichert challenges teachers to just blindly reach out to someone. Many times, he has made a phone call or sent an email and have been met with positive responses. Most businesses and companies want to collaborate, provide opportunities, and give donations. Businesses and local companies also talk to each other and will recommend partnering with the CTE program. Being able to tap into their wealth of resources provides once in a lifetime opportunities to students and builds a strong pipeline. Being able to see the overall picture and know what you are capable of handling is the key, but even more so is having students that want to be involved and complete these projects. Students need to be professional and capable before committing to projects. Understanding their skills and what they can accomplish is critical to a successful partnership. Using industry-recognized credentials also help students gain important content knowledge, level up their learning, and help promote them upon graduation.

Outside of the classroom, Reichert has created the Sunrise Skilled Trades Camp to open opportunities to students in grades 10–12 to learn about the skilled trades. Harbor Freight Tools for Schools, Wyoming Department of Education, and a few other donors help provide this free opportunity to students. This camp is open to students around the country. For the week of camp, students get to help remodel the YMCA in a small mining town. Each day, there are different competitions where campers can win a variety of prizes and scheduling evening activities for students to have fun. All campers receive a t-shirt, all meals, tools, and protective equipment. Reichert hopes to go even more nationwide with the camp and hopes to continue increasing the opportunities.

Reichert hopes that CTE teachers understand his big takeaways:

- Relationships are everything. Being in tune with your students and focusing on their learning is the key to success. Relationships with businesses also create opportunities for students and give back to the community. Focus on the students and community you are in.
- Let people know who you are. Don't try to be someone else.
- Be honest with students.
- Focus on being a mentor.

Moving forward, Reichert aims to deepen his efforts in delivering authentic learning, solidifying a lasting impact. He wants to expand the pipeline from school to work for students.

The journey from assigning conventional essays to championing authentic learning projects has been a transformative one, fueled by a desire for students to own their education and connect it to the real world. By prioritizing projects that align with industry practices, integrate diverse skills, and serve a genuine audience, educators can move beyond the limitations of traditional instruction. Whether through video essays, podcasts, industry-aligned scenarios, community partnerships, or interdisciplinary collaborations, the goal remains consistent: to cultivate critical thinkers, problem-solvers, and confident communicators ready for their future careers. While challenges like time and resources may arise, starting small and fostering robust communication with supervisors and community partners can pave the way for impactful, student-driven experiences. Ultimately, by shifting the focus from mere content consumption to active creation and real-world application, educators empower students to discover deeper meaning in their work, sparking the excitement that truly defines successful and lasting learning.

Frederick W. Smith wrote a term paper for his college class about ways to accommodate time-sensitive shipments and received an average grade. While this assignment was based on solving a real problem, it sparked an entire company. Smith went on to create Fedex (FeDEx, n.d.). Michele Perkins was teaching her fellow peers design during college and grew frustrated with the tools available. This frustration sparked creating a more accessible program. As she evolved her company, she was told no more than 100 times and investors didn't believe in her. Today, her company Canva, has 90 million monthly users and generates $1 billion in annual revenue (Hinchliffe, 2022). You can never underestimate the influence and impact you will have on a student. One assignment, one challenge, and one moment can spark an entire company. Providing students with the opportunity to engage in solving complex problems and even dreaming big can lead to amazing results. Our world today reflects that age has no limits in success. At the age of 13, Shubham Banerjee built a Braille printer with a Lego robotics kit for a school science fair project (Chea, 2015). Banerjee was able to continue working on his project, securing funding from investors and starting his own company leading to his success (Shubham Banerjee, n.d.). The stories of Frederick Smith, Melanie Perkins, and Shubham Banerjee are not just inspiring anecdotes; they are a profound testament to the power of a single idea and the potential that resides within every student. In each case, a classroom assignment or a simple project served as the fertile ground for innovation, ultimately leading to the creation of companies that have changed industries and the world. Your assignments have the power to change the future of the world.

**Recommended Reading**

- *Authentic Learning Real-World Experiences That Build 21st-Century Skill* by Todd Stanley.
- *Designing Authentic Performance Tasks and Projects: Tools for Meaningful Learning and Assessment* by Jay McTighe, Kristina J, Doubet, Eric M. Carbaugh.
- *Hacking Project Based Learning: 10 Easy Steps to PBL and Inquiry in the Classroom* by Ross Cooper and Erin Murphy.

 **Discussion Questions**

- How can you define what authentic learning will look like in your classroom?
- As you consider integrating more authentic learning, what specific, personal challenges or anxieties do you anticipate facing? What *first steps* could you take to proactively mitigate one of these anticipated hurdles?
- Beyond a traditional report or test, what does a "product" truly mean in the context of an authentic learning experience in *your specific CTE program*?
- Looking ahead, what is one authentic learning experience you dream of bringing into your CTE classroom? What steps would you need to take (resources, partnerships, personal learning) to make that dream a reality for your students?

## References

Career and Technical Student Organizations. (2024, July 17). *National Coordinating Council for Career and Technical Student Organizations Definition, Mission, Purpose and Criteria for Membership*. www.

ctsos.org/wp-content/uploads/2019/03/2016-Final-Definition-NCC-CTS-JULY-16.pdf

Chea, T. (2015). *This 13-Year-Old Started A Company After Building A Braille Printer With Legos.* Business Insider. www.businessinsider.com/this-13-year-old-started-a-company-after-building-a-braille-printer-with-legos-2015-1

DECA. (n.d.). *Our Mission.* DECA.org. Retrieved July 24, 2025. www.deca.org/mission

FeDEx. (n.d.). https://www.fedex.com/en-us/about/history.html

Hinchliffe. (n.d.). https://fortune.com/2024/05/24/canva-ceo-melanie-perkins-comes-to-the-u-s-to-woo-the-design-businesss-next-generation-of-enterprise-clients/

Lucas Education Research. (n.d.). The Evidence is Clear: Rigorous Project-Based Learning is an Effective Lever for Student Success. *Rigorous Project-Based Learning.* Lucas Education Research. www.lucasedresearch.org/wp-content/uploads/2021/04/Research-Summary-of-PBL-Rev1-1.pdf

PBL Works. (n.d.-a). Gold Standard: Project Design Elements. PBL Works. Retrieved July 18, 2025. www.pblworks.org/what-is-pbl/gold-standard-project-designs

PBL Works. (n.d.-b). What is Project Based Learning? | PBLWorks. PBL Works. Retrieved July 18, 2025. www.pblworks.org/what-is-pbl

PBLWorks. (n.d.). *Project Walls | MyPBLWorks.* myPBLWorks. Retrieved July 18, 2025. https://my.pblworks.org/resource/pbl_project_wall

Shubham Banerjee. (n.d.). https://www.shu.today/

SkillsUSA. (n.d.). *Foundational History.* SkillsUSA. Retrieved July 24, 2025. www.skillsusa.org/who-we-are/history/

Stanley, T. (2018). *Authentic Learning: Real-World Experiences That Build 21st-Century Skills.* Prufrock Press.

# 4

# Work-Based Learning Experiences

My student and I sat huddled around her cell phone. We took turns pressing the mute button to discuss an answer to a question as the person on the other side of the phone was talking. We were having a conference call with a potential internship placement, and my student was extremely nervous. By the end of the call, the student had secured a placement with the occupational therapy group and was extremely excited about the opportunities she was going to be given. The cornerstone of a quality CTE program is work-based learning (WBL). We need to prepare our students to be job-ready by the time they leave our school system. WBL is more than just providing internship/work experiences to students. It is careful planning and building of employability skills and a continuum of learning for the student. The World Economic Forum projects that 39% of worker's exciting skill sets will be transformed or outdated over the next 5 years (World Economic Forum, 2025). This startling fact makes it clear that we must urgently prepare our students with the skills they will need to thrive in a rapidly evolving economy.

The National Center for College and Career recommends a continuum where the WBL program starts early with students increasing their career awareness, builds by career exploration, and ends with career preparation (2021). Setting goals early for students and a support team creates a comprehensive and successful program. It also helps students develop soft skills to navigate changing landscapes. At a federal level, the Perkins Initiative identifies three key components of WBL programs. First, there is an alignment of classroom and workplace learning, next there is an application of academic, technical skills in work-based settings, and lastly, there is support from mentors in both the workplace and classroom (Work-Based Learning (WBL) Tool Kit, n.d.). The integrated approach ensures students are not only learning but also actively preparing for their future.

At the core, WBL provides students with various opportunities to experience careers. There are different types of WBL. The following are some of the most common WBL experiences:

- Career Assessments/Leadership Style Assessments
    - Many companies offer career assessments that students can take to understand how their skills, personality, and interests are aligned with different career paths. Similarly, different types of assessments can measure what leadership style a student is, personality assessments, and even communication styles.
    - Each test provides insights that students can use to consider a different perspective or understand themselves better.
- Guest Speakers
    - Professionals from the industry visit the classroom to share insights with students, more on guest speakers in Chapter 6.
- Workplace Tours/Field Trips
    - Going outside the classroom to see operations in action, observing professionals performing their duties, and gaining a holistic sense of the work environment are important for students. The sensory experience of being immersed in the workplace is something the classroom can't replicate. Students can visualize the big picture and see beyond the job description. Tours also provide a realistic, firsthand look into the career, often dispelling myths and overcoming misconceptions.

- Job Shadowing
  - Students are paired with industry professionals and observe the day-to-day responsibilities. This typically is a 1-day experience.
- School-Based Enterprise
  - This is a student-run business located within the school. Students typically take on roles to produce goods or services for the students, staff, or community. This could be a school store, auto repairs, or a cosmetology clinic.
- Community Service/Service Learning
  - Service learning is the process of learning through volunteer work. Some types of service learning include tutoring, helping conduct research, and creating public information campaigns for a community.
- Internship
  - Internships are experiences that focus on giving students hands-on experiences in the field. They can be paid or unpaid, and students sometimes receive academic credit.
- Cooperative Education Experience
  - Co-ops are structured programs where students alternate between academic studies and full-time work. They are longer-term.
- Apprenticeship
  - Pre-apprenticeship/Youth Apprenticeship
    - These are the traditional programs that provide on-the-job training and guidance under a mentor. Typically, they lead to nationally recognized credentials. Youth or pre-apprenticeships are for high school students to prepare them to enter a full apprenticeship program.
- Clinical Experience
  - Supervised clinical experiences allow students to work with patients and in real-world settings. This is often required for licensing or certifications. This is common with healthcare, teaching, and cosmetology.

If a school has a WBL program, it will also have a dedicated employee who oversees the internships. Each district is different, but working closely with that person helps students be successful in completing the internship/WBL experience. You will work closely with the internship or WBL coordinator when students are completing their internships. The coordinators usually oversee the following:

- Visiting internship sites and assessing safety.
- Documenting internship hours.
- Communicating with partners about the program.
- Overseeing student performance.

It is important to understand how your school coordinates internships. Ask questions. The first year I taught CTE, I scheduled a meeting with my WBL coordinator and barely remembered anything. I took a ton of notes and sat with the information because I asked many follow-up questions. Even when I felt my questions were silly or I should know the information, I still grew the courage to ask. Don't be afraid to ask for another meeting.

Being strategic about how to manage a WBL program that builds on student skills and ultimately prepares them for the workforce is critical. Similar to teaching new concepts to students, teachers should carefully plan WBL experiences to support students in building responsibility and accountability. This means that starting in grade 9, students are exposed to the industry, learn foundations, and interact with guest speakers. Students should meet the WBL coordinator, and they should speak to your students a few times throughout the year. It can be a fun activity about applying for jobs, public speaking, or interviewing. Continue that relationship throughout sophomore year and junior year. Each year can include more activities that build on each other. During junior year, focusing on building experiences for students to see the industry create a successful partnership. By the time they are approaching junior year, they are taking initiative in talking to different businesses, applying for internships during their senior year, and taking control of their own job experience. Senior year, students should be in internship/WBL experiences. Strategically having activities and lessons that build on each other from year to year enriches a student's experience while building capacity in that student. Creating such interdependence on activities provides students the chance to mature, learn essential skills, and create relationships. Preparing students for the internship during their senior year should start when students first enter the school. Students will inevitably be working with guest speakers, advisory council members, and the community. By fostering professionalism early, students will be more successful in securing high-quality internships.

Consider creating a timeline of WBL experiences for students as they enter your CTE program.

| Grade 9 | ♦ Teach basic foundations and skills for students to succeed<br>♦ Collaborate with WBL coordinators once a marking period for students to gain exposure and start thinking about internships<br>♦ Career fair hosted by students<br>♦ Career pathway research<br>♦ What credentials, skills, and training do students need?<br>♦ Industry guest speakers<br>♦ Workplace tours<br>♦ Basic industry safety certifications |
|---|---|
| Grade 10 | ♦ Portfolio building<br>♦ Resume building and skills inventory<br>♦ Simulated workplace scenarios<br>♦ Industry challenge projects<br>♦ Industry guest speakers and collaborations |
| Grade 11 | ♦ Have monthly visits with the WBL coordinator<br>♦ Have students create resumes and cover letters<br>♦ Mock interviews<br>♦ Research for life after high school<br>♦ Professional communication workshops<br>   ♦ Email etiquette<br>   ♦ Elevator pitch<br>♦ Job shadowing |

| Grade 12 | ♦ WBL coordinator oversees site visits and communicates progress<br>♦ Capstone project<br>   ♦ Consider the seniors returning back to speak to the younger grades about their experience<br>♦ Networking event/career fair<br>♦ Certification exams |
|---|---|

    Some businesses/organizations may be hesitant to work with a high school to provide internship experience. There may also be an age requirement and restrictions on what students can do. Meet businesses where they are at their level of comfort. Start with a guest speaking opportunity, and show the business your students in action. For example, a local occupational therapy group started by being a guest speaker for students to learn about the profession. After 2 years of being a guest speaker and working with the students, they were open to the idea of having an intern. Always be open to making any type of relationship work, as it could open doors later on for students. It could be beneficial to have a one-page brag sheet about your students/program that can be sent out when making partnerships. Included in it should be any skills your students have, certifications, work experience, and program information. Be clear about any time commitments students need to obtain. Don't count a business out just because they said no at first. Work on the relationship, and over time, the business could come around. Businesses are eager to help, but also need to worry about legal liability.

    As noted earlier, some programs require a certain number of hours for students to complete as part of graduation. When planning for students to complete their required hours for graduation, give students a guide. For example, each month the student should aim to complete a certain number of hours. Create a mock schedule for students to follow. This schedule would outline when they are attending their classes, internships, and free time. Students are juggling work, sports, clubs, familial commitments, and being a student, they are also still learning how to properly manage their time. Creating mock schedules during junior year and learning how to prioritize will not only help them successfully finish their internship but also teach them valuable life skills. Each school has a different WBL model and senior year model. Regardless of your school's model, build regular check-ins with your students. The WBL coordinator typically goes on-site visits and works one on one with the students. Each CTE school has its own model for senior year. In some schools, students have WBL for certain blocks each day but still attend CTE classes. In other schools, students will attend the local community college for their senior year and not come to the high school campus. Other schools might use a hybrid model of the mentioned ways. If you don't teach students during their senior year because they attend the college option, you might be tasked with facilitating monthly check-ins with your students to help students continue to have a relationship with the school and CTE program. Since students are going to be giving up their time to come to school, be sure to make the meetings purposeful for the students. Some ideas are as follows:

- Have students share out and reflect on things they have learned at their internship or college.
- Give each meeting a dedicated topic to explore; this can include post-secondary options, finances after graduation, meeting with local professional organizations, capstone projects, resumes, applying to college, finding scholarships, and much more.
- Encourage students to bring real-world challenges and questions they've encountered at their internship. Students can offer advice, resources, or similar experiences.

If your school doesn't have this type of model, setting aside specific time for students to discuss their WBL opportunities and explore post-secondary options is valuable.

Summer is another opportunity for students to complete their internship hours. Students can work more hours during the day to see daily operations and a glimpse of the job. Some schools only allow students to complete a specific number of hours during the summer. With more time on site, students have greater opportunities to take on more complex tasks, participate in larger projects, and develop a wider range of technical and soft skills. They can move beyond shadowing to actively contributing to the workplace. Businesses are often more willing to take on student interns during the summer when their own operations might be running at a different pace or when they have more capacity for training and mentorship without the constraints of a student's academic schedule. Encourage students to start their search early, leverage school resources (WBL coordinator, counselors), and utilize personal networks.

Creating a handbook for students, parents, and mentors with clear expectations, outlined responsibilities, important dates, and more provides transparency for each person involved in the process. It also shows a level of accountability for each person. Check with your WBL coordinator if your school or state has a handbook. Consider making your own handbook or even guide to WBL experiences; you can share with potential internship placements or students if your school doesn't provide one. This should include as follows:

Clear definition of WBL and its purpose
Goals and benefits to the community and the student
Table of Contents
Student Section
  Eligibility Requirements
   Academic criteria (if applicable)
   Attendance requirements
- Application Process
  - Steps on how students apply for a WBL placement
  - Any required forms
- Student Responsibilities and Expectations
  - Professional conduct
  - Workplace ethics
  - Any documentation requirements
- Safety and Compliance
  - Child Labor Laws
  - Confidentiality notice
  - Conflict resolution process

- Assessment and Evaluation
  - How students are assessed

Parent/Guardian Section
    What is WBL?
    Roles and Responsibilities of Parents/Guardians
    Consent forms

Employer Section
    Welcome to the Program
    Benefits of Hosting a WBL Student
    Roles and Responsibilities of the Employer
        Providing a safe, productive, and supervised learning experience
        Assigning a workplace mentor
        Communicating with WBL coordinator
        Providing regular feedback
    Safety and Compliance
        Child Labor Laws
        Understanding liability
    Evaluation Process

A well-structured WBL handbook provides essential information but demonstrates the professionalism and commitment of the school to providing high-quality, safe, and meaningful WBL opportunities.

As the senior students complete their internship experience, invite them to speak to the younger students in the program. Providing the younger students insight into their internship experience provides a real look into the industry experiences and resonates deeply while providing concrete examples of their future. Seniors can create a presentation or host a talk about the following:

- Internship/WBL Experience
  - Overview of the experience – Where was the internship? What was their role and the overall scope of the work?
  - Responsibilities within the internship – A look into the day-to-day duties and specific projects they contributed to

- ♦ Points of challenge/areas of growth – Share obstacles they face and how they learned to overcome them, highlighting resilience
♦ Next Steps
  - ♦ Next steps and plans – Discuss how the experience has shaped postgraduation plans.
  - ♦ Takeaways of the overall experience – What surprising insights did they gain about the industry, workplace culture, or their own strengths?
  - ♦ Advice in planning for senior year – Provide younger students with practical tips on preparing for WBL and senior year.

For CTE programs that offer dual enrollment, seniors can expand on their college-level experiences, discussing coursework, campus life, and how it connects to their career goals. When seniors share their experiences, it reinforces the learning for the seniors themselves.

## Ways to Support Students Before Their Internship

As the CTE teacher, there are many ways to support students in preparing them for internships. Being purposeful in how you are preparing students for internships links back to lesson planning best practices.

### Guest Speakers
Guest speakers provide a glimpse into the industry, and exploratory activities to understand different careers within an industry allow students to begin thinking of their future careers. See Chapter 6 to explore more on guest speakers.

### Work Ethic and Responsibility
Discuss the importance of punctuality, reliability, initiative, and a strong work ethic. Assign tasks that require independent follow-through and adherence to deadlines. Help students understand that showing up on time and prepared, taking

notes, and following instructions are fundamental expectations. Give students different ethical scenarios and discuss how they would react and common ways to handle when things go wrong. Another option is creating a project document that outlines a project and day-to-day responsibilities. Students will need to practice prioritizing how they would complete a project and complete all their responsibilities.

**How to Navigate the Job Market**
Preparing our students to interview well starts with deliberate preparation. In this multistep lesson, I teach students how to look for job posts, evaluate job posts, sort through resumes, and address job market misconceptions.

- Searching for Jobs
  For students, they may be unaware of the best place to look for when searching for a job or internship. With so many different platforms, it is easy to get lost and miss potential jobs. Equally important is teaching students to read job descriptions carefully. Pick a platform that is commonly used to find jobs in your specific industry. You can start by picking one job description and having your students evaluate it. Common questions for students to look for as they do this are as follows:
- What is the core purpose of this role?
- What are the main responsibilities? Are they clearly defined?
- What specific skills or knowledge is the company looking for?
- Are there specific software, tools, or certifications the company is looking for?
- What does the job description reveal about the culture of the company? Are there any red flags?
  While most people are eager to find a job, having students be confident about finding a career instead of a temporary job is important. We want our students to learn how to look for places where they will thrive.

- Analyzing Resumes
- To simulate what a hiring director might see, I wanted my students to gain a new perspective on their own resumes and cover letters. Using AI, I created four resumes of highly qualified candidates that were applying to a real job description. I split my students into four groups. Each group received a different resume that I created. In these groups, they carefully evaluated the resume. Students needed to evaluate the strengths and weaknesses of the resume and the candidate.
- After students had an opportunity to discuss and get to know their candidate, I switched their groups again. This time, each person in the group had a different resume. I tell students they have been tasked with hiring a candidate for the job description. They need to work together to pick one of the candidates. I have students create a protocol for sharing their candidates and discussing. This eliminates the "my candidate should be hired because I said so". They asked each other probing questions, defended their chosen candidates, thoroughly explored résumés, and drew clear connections between the job description's requirements and their candidates' qualifications. These discussions were more than just a debate; they were a rich opportunity for students to hone their leadership abilities and practice advocating for their perspectives. Crucially, the exercise also fostered resilience, as students navigated the give-and-take of real-world decision-making and, at times, demonstrated the maturity to admit when their initial candidate might not be the absolute best fit for the role after considering all viewpoints.
- Students felt confident by the end of the exercise. It also led to great learning points about how to navigate life changes on a resume. One resume had a person who didn't have any relevant experience but did have retail experience. Another resume had someone who took a few years off from work. I wanted students to be aware

that not every resume is going to look the same, and it's okay when certain life events happen.

## Email Communications

I am surprised each year when I have to explain what cc and bcc mean to students. I always assume they know, and some do, but I have to teach them when to use cc versus a bcc. Teaching students about professionalism and how to communicate is important. While students may have heard a similar speech before, students need to know your expectations. Explicitly teach students that emails should have a formal salutation, a nice greeting, information on the program, and the internship ask. Students need to close with a professional signature.

Students need to be taught how to organize their emails and continuously check them. Often, students go into "coast" mode, where they ignore everything because they think it is all "junk" from the school about different events going on.

## Mock Interviews

Conducting interview scenarios or mock job practicals is important. It provides students with an opportunity to discuss how to dress, how to answer questions, and what questions to ask. Beyond just answering questions, students learn *how* to articulate their skills and experiences clearly, concisely, and persuasively. They practice active listening and develop the ability to ask insightful questions, demonstrating their engagement and critical thinking. Invite advisory council members, parents, or other staff to interview your students. Share questions that are most commonly asked in interviews so students can prepare answers. If you aren't the best interview person, consider working with your WBL coordinator to help your students.

This past year, I invited administration to interview my students for a mock role in the administration team. My students spent several days thinking of different answers to common interview questions, creating an elevator pitch, and discussing best practices in interviewing. We even discussed what to wear for an interview. This knowledge is sometimes assumed but as the teacher, we should avoid making assumptions about what students know. When the students finally interviewed with the administrators, they were beyond nervous. After the interview, they received feedback from the administrators based on a rubric I provided to them. By integrating these robust interview preparation strategies, you're not just teaching content; you're equipping students with the indispensable soft skills and confidence needed to navigate the competitive world of job applications and secure valuable internship opportunities.

### Elevator Pitch Practice

I found myself at a conference trying to find a company that would allow my students to earn credentials and certificates in the education space without being a certified teacher. Many companies were excited about the work I was doing, but didn't see how the partnership could work. After the first day of defeat, I had to rework my pitch. It dawned on me, I needed an elevator pitch that was well-rehearsed and captured what I wanted to share about my students. After really thinking about and carefully planning what I wanted to say, I was able to find a company that wanted to take on my vision with me. The elevator pitch may seem like a mundane practice, but it does serve an important purpose. You never know when you will find yourself in the presence of someone who might want to hire you, partner with you, or give you money for your program. Having a rehearsed speech that captures everything is an important skill.

Provide your students with a template to create an elevator pitch. Have your students practice the pitch. Give them feedback. The Career Development Center at Princeton University (n.d.) recommends asking a question at the end to engage the other person. This makes the elevator pitch more of a conversation instead of a sales pitch leading to better connections.

### Phone Call Practice

To order a pizza, you don't even need to call someone. There are probably five different services that will bring it to you just by clicking a few buttons on your cell phone. Picking up a phone and calling another human can be a scary process for students.

Have students practice calling a place of business and talking to someone over the phone.

## Social Media Presence

As we know, technology surrounds us. Teens are using social media to post pictures, get information, and engage with others. Since the brain isn't developed yet and humans make mistakes, teens don't always make the best decisions online. It is not our job to lecture about social media, but we do have a duty to talk about employability skills. If teens leave their social media accounts for public display, industry partners might see their content. We must tell students potential consequences if they post inappropriate videos, photos, or statements. Most schools give students their own email accounts. Some students will change their account picture on their school account to something funny or sometimes inappropriate. Reminding students as they start to email industry professionals to double-check their accounts is important.

A dedicated social media page for your CTE program can be an incredibly powerful asset, offering a dynamic platform to highlight achievements and engage with various stakeholders. Depending on your school's specific social media policies and guidelines, a well-managed page can serve multiple vital functions. The social media page can serve as a marketing tool, providing prospective students and their families with compelling visual narratives of what your program offers. For local businesses and potential advisory council members, the page serves as a window into practical skills your students are developing.

Always operate strictly within your school district's social media policies. Ensure all students have submitted photo release forms that are signed by parents/guardians. Do not follow students' personal accounts on the program page. As the teacher, it is important to maintain a professional, educational focus. Running social media does have advantages but you also need to be consistent in posting.

## Stackable Credentials or Industry-Recognized Credentials

If we are truly preparing students to enter the world after high school graduation, students need the right experiences and, more importantly, credentials. Credentials are evidence of an individual's qualifications for a particular task. A professional credential is given to individuals when they master specific knowledge against a set of accepted industry standards. Different professional associations may offer credentials. For example, the Occupational Safety and Health Administration (OSHA) is a federal agency within the U.S. Department of Labor. OSHA sets safety standards and provides training. Many CTE schools will have their students complete OSHA 10 certification, so students can be eligible to work with a wide range of companies. More importantly, it focuses on workplace safety. Students understand the importance of workplace safety and start their training with safety as the foundation. There are many other nationally recognized credentials that CTE teachers can have their students complete.

As the industry expert, you probably have some idea of the different credentials students can earn. If you aren't sure, use different resources like your state's CTE page, where there is typically a list of recommended credentials. You can also try a Google Search, looking for different companies to contact, or you can contact other CTE teachers in the area. You can also consider embedding credentials into your curriculum. For example, during my unit on designing curriculum, students take the UDL Mindset Credential 1. This unit happens during their sophomore year. Students continue to move through other credentials and earn several before graduation their senior year.

Beyond the diploma, credentials act as a powerful signal to employers. In a competitive job market, credentials show students have specific, job-ready skills and can set them apart from other candidates. Further, credentials are typically nationally recognized and portable. Students aren't confined to a certain region but can explore many options and have a common industry language.

Teachers should consider scaffolding different credentials throughout their program. Once identified, embedding credentials directly into your curriculum is a powerful strategy. This means structuring lessons and projects in a way that naturally prepares students for the credentialing exam, making it a logical culmination of their learning, rather than an add-on. Badges/micro-credentials are becoming more common and focus on competence in a very specific skill. They typically take less time to complete, but are just as impactful. Credentials are important because they are typically nationally recognized and verify that individuals have a certain level of skill. Credentials can help students secure a job and apply for a higher-paying job.

**Finding Internships**
It is important to understand the expectations of the school and its WBL program. Some schools want students to identify their own internships and seek the opportunity. This will include the student reaching out and communicating with the business. Other schools provide a list of internship placements that students can choose from. Regardless of the expectations of your school, keep a list of all contacts and partners for internships. These possible internship partners can serve as guest speakers, thought partners, and advisory board council members.

If students do need to contact the internships, it is important to spend time reviewing email etiquette. Providing a template or guidelines is important. Oftentimes, students will use the school's name or your name as credibility. If you want your name and school to have a good reputation, teaching students explicitly how to talk about potential opportunities is important.

Some internship sites require special permission/testing to work at certain internships. Most of my students are all interns in public schools. Some of the schools require students to complete their fingerprints, a tuberculosis shot, and/or complete a background check. They also have to be board-approved. Other examples of requirements for internships are being OSHA 10 or OSHA 30 certified, a certain age (some businesses require students to be 17 or 18), a driver's license, or certain certifications. When students communicate and apply for an internship, they should be aware of whether certain businesses have requirements. It can also help you in recommending places to students if they need to be of a certain age.

Students are often responsible for their transportation to their internships. If students have a hard time with transportation, think about local businesses within walking distance of the school and public transportation. Internships can be paid or unpaid, depending on the place of employment. Students will need to have an assigned mentor at the internship who will provide the student with feedback. Typically, students can attend their internship at the same time and days each week.

As the teacher for the program, you can ask your administrator for time during the day to go to a potential partner for an internship and a guest speaker to vet them. Student safety is obviously most important and key. Being able to walk around the place of business and seeing where students could be working provides a sense of safety.

In communicating with the businesses, ask pointed questions about the work the student will be engaging in. Will the placement offer genuine learning and skill application? If students are spending their time, you want the work to be meaningful and relevant, not just busy work. Ensure that the students will be able to engage in rigorous work-site activities. Students should be able to contribute significantly to the workplace. They should not be just doing basic work like filing papers, bringing coffee to bosses, or running errands.

## Mentors

When students are completing an internship, they will need to have an assigned mentor. The mentor plays a pivotal role in helping students serve as a bridge between theory and real-world practice. They provide guidance, support, and a deeper understanding. They should be ready to help students with transitioning into the workplace, giving students feedback on their work, demonstrating techniques, and offering advice. As students learn from their mentors, students can expand their industry knowledge. Mentors share their insights into industry trends, best practices, challenges, and opportunities. Mentors serve as the first networking experience students have that is beyond the classroom experience. Their internship is the first step in expanding their network and opening doors to future opportunities.

Typically, WBL programs have a mentor handbook that mentors need to sign. The mentor handbook should be developed by your WBL coordinator or school to ensure each program is aligned. However, the handbook should outline expectations of the program, any evaluations the mentor needs to complete, types of learning experiences being offered, and important contact information.

## Barriers to Overcome

### Students Not Performing Well

Environments are extremely important for growth. Emily, a high school senior, emailed me saying she was struggling at her internship. She was working in an elementary school with a 4th-grade class. I suggested we meet to discuss what was happening and find a solution. When we first got on the video call to discuss, I let Emily tell me what was going on. She felt her mentor was giving her too much work and expected too much from her. After I let Emily vent about her internship, I was completely honest with her. She needed to ask more questions of her mentor for clarity, but Emily also had to take a risk and try teaching a class. Emily had to go through a productive struggle with her internship to ultimately grow. By the end of the call, Emily accepted the responsibility and said she would try the different strategies we discussed. In reflecting on this experience, I thought about my own communication with Emily and her peers. I think I failed to communicate the expectations of the internship.

Unfortunately, some students may struggle during their senior year. They can struggle for a variety of reasons, like failing to meet expectations, being overwhelmed with the workload, or family problems. A medical issue can cause a student to miss their internship and school for extended periods of time. Students may not be a good fit for certain companies, bosses, or colleagues. The WBL coordinator may be the contact person with the mentor assigned to your student. If students are struggling to meet the expectations of the internship, it is important to support the student and evaluate the student's placement.

When talking to students about their struggles, be open to listening. Sometimes students just need to say their problems out loud to solve them. If students are struggling, the WBL coordinator and school counselor are good supports for the student. Be sure to continue to check in on the student.

### Businesses Not Being Great Partners

Similar to our own working experiences, there will be times when a mentor or business/organization isn't the best partner. This could look like mistreating the student, inappropriate business practices, or miscommunication. If students communicate that they feel uncomfortable or unsafe in their internship, contact your WBL coordinator and supervisor. This may look like a conversation between the WBL coordinator and internship mentor. Be sure to tell students they need to document any incidents or concerns with specifics, which would include times, specific actions, and any previous attempts to resolve the issue. Addressing these situations might involve a conversation between your WBL coordinator and the internship mentor to clarify expectations, resolve misunderstandings, or, if necessary, reevaluate the partnership. Our goal is to ensure a safe, productive, and valuable learning experience for all students.

### Equitable Access

Unfortunately, as WBL continues to grow across the nation, there are several growing pains. Currently, each state has its own model and resources for WBL. This fragmented landscape means that the quality and availability of WBL opportunities can vary wildly from one state or even one district to another. To mitigate these challenges, there's a growing need for greater collaboration among states, sharing of successful models, and the development of national best practices or guidelines to ensure all students have equitable access to valuable WBL experiences.

In a report by the New Skills Ready Network, the authors explore how to address equity blockers to WBL. Students having access to transportation is key for attending a WBL experience. Public transportation is a great option if the work sites are near a route. If students do not own a car and have access to reliable transportation, they are less likely to participate. The financial needs of a student would discourage students from participating in the WBL experience. Students often choose not to participate in WBL experiences aligned with their career pathway to accept a job that pays a higher wage. Another reason students chose not to participate in WBL was due to a lack of professional attire and access to materials. Typically, students will need a uniform, professional dress clothes, or supplies to start an experience. Again, the financial burden or lack of knowledge of resources prevented students from participating (New Skills Ready Network, n.d.).

There are many different states, organizations, and companies looking for solutions to provide more equitable access so students can participate. To combat some inequities and make WBL better, consider developing a range of high-quality WBL implementation models (New Skills Ready Network, n.d.). A school in Dallas created a Virtual Internship Toolkit to increase opportunities for students. Boston Public Schools partnered with the Boston Private Industry Council to partner in pairing employers in the same industry to create support networks. While you may not be in a position to change wages, provide transportation, or create companies, there are several steps you can take to help provide equitable access. First, developing robust data collection systems works to identify equity issues in your district and school. Consider what information you would like to gather from students to better help serve them. This information can be presented to your supervisor to help create solutions. Next, identify partners in your industry that are already working with your students. Are there ways to deepen or expand these existing partnerships? Talk to your current industry contacts and collaboratively explore solutions they might offer to broaden access, such as creating more flexible schedules, offering virtual components, or connecting you with other businesses in their network committed to diversity. Remember that the core of your impact lies in your daily interactions. By maintaining high expectations for all students, proactively seeking out diverse learning opportunities, and consistently connecting students with relevant resources (even if that's just a conversation with a school counselor), you dismantle barriers one student at a time.

## Student Spotlight

Hudson Darmanin was in the culinary kitchen, sifting through various green vegetables, working on his independent study. Hudson spent countless hours in the kitchen working on his various skills. When I first met Hudson, he was a senior in high school and had just finished his internship at Summit House in New Jersey and was currently working at Gramercy Tavern in New York City.

His parents originally approached him about the idea of attending his county's CTE school because it ranked higher than his town's high school. Hudson had a desire to pursue Culinary Arts and was really interested in fine-dining restaurants. Hudson credits his CTE teacher's efforts to harvest and cultivate his interests to his success. His teacher lent him cookbooks to take him and gave Hudson a choice in projects. He said he was able to learn more because his teacher incorporated choice into the curriculum. When his CTE teacher approached him about completing his internship in a fine-dining restaurant, Hudson was excited.

Hudson's most valuable learning experiences were during his internship and the opportunity to create a three-course menu that he had to cook for a panel of school administrators. He was able to think about menu design, how each dish was crafted and paired. He took each thing he learned from both the Summit House and Gramercy Tavern to create his own menu.

Hudson offers invaluable advice for new CTE teachers, rooted in his transformative experiences:

- Listen to your students and share stories: Hudson loved being able to hear Chef's stories from the industry and relate them to his own experiences during his internship. These stories resonated with him and provided a shared sense of a journey.
- Empower through choice: He also appreciated having a choice. If the curriculum were a one-size-fits-all approach, he thinks his love for culinary would have been diminished quickly.
- Embrace diverse WBL opportunities: The various WBL opportunities throughout his high school career also helped shape him. For example, during his freshman and sophomore years, his class had to make and serve breakfast at county meetings. His culinary teacher also brought them to the Culinary Institute of America to visualize themselves there after high school.

Hudson is now attending the Culinary Institute of America, where he is excited to continue his educational journey and one day own his own restaurant. Hudson shared candidly about working in environments where he was consistently surrounded by professionals with significantly more experience than himself. He was tasked with leading a prep team and needed to manage people effectively while also treating them with the same respect and hospitality that was embedded in the Union Square Hospitality Group. During his time there, he was promoted to preparing complex purées and sauces. He honed in on his efficiency, and he used many of the skills his chef taught him during his CTE program. Lastly, Hudson underscored the immense value of networking and mentorship, actively seeking and taking advice from every professional he encountered, underscoring the collaborative nature of the culinary world.

## End of Internship/WBL Project Ideas

As students complete their internships, they should be constantly reflecting on their internships and learning. A culminating project can demonstrate their growth over the year. It also holds students accountable for their time and allows you to assess the program.

- Capstone
  A capstone project acts as the grand finale that showcases everything a student has learned throughout their CTE program. Capstone projects rely heavily on the practical application of the skills and knowledge learned and are designed to address real-world problems. The project is student-led in which students define a problem, develop solutions, and manage the project. One example is a carpentry class building a shed for the local public works to store tools and equipment.
- Portfolio
  Requiring seniors to complete a portfolio as a final project can help students be ready to take on any job and reflect on all their hard work. A portfolio is a collection of artifacts that the student gathers. Students can create a website that serves as their portfolio and can be linked to their resume. They can also continue to update their portfolio as they move through their next steps after high school.
- Possible Requirements:
  - Personal Statement
  - Resume
  - Reference Page
  - Certifications
  - Examples of Work
  - Honors/Achievements
  - Volunteer Experience
  - Extra Curricular Activities
  - Writing/Research Samples
  - SMART Goals/5-Year Plan
- Senior Showcase
  Completing a CTE program and internship is a huge accomplishment. A senior showcase is a class-wide event

where seniors can present their internships, next steps, and reflect on their growth. Students can prepare a presentation or trifold and host a table for parents, community members, businesses, and teachers to visit. This celebration of hard work and highlighting learning inspires all to continue working toward the goal of CTE, to provide comprehensive, real-world opportunities for students.

◆ Signing Ceremony

To celebrate the end of the CTE program and highlight students' next steps, some high schools have hosted signing ceremonies. When students are committing to a college for sports, there is typically a signing ceremony with the college, high school, and student. If students have a signed contract to continue working after graduation, this would be part of the signing ceremony. This would also apply if students are entering an apprentice program, trade school, or college with a major in their CTE field. It also serves as a motivator for younger students to watch. If you want to host a signing ceremony, make it a big deal! Send invitations for parents, businesses, and other teachers to attend. Students can sign their contract in a ceremony. It also provides a nice photo opportunity for students to remember where their career started.

In looking at different states' WBL programs, the Kansas Department of Education offers an employability skills assessment that the internship mentor can complete for the student. It highlights how students are performing in three different categories: effective relationships, workplace skills, and applied knowledge (Kansas Work-Based Learning: Personalized Learning Plan Guidance Document, 2019). They also offer the same skills assessment for students to complete and a reflection sheet.

Kansas was one of ten states featured in a report by the American Student Assistance, sharing stories of states making progress in WBL. Kansas created a regional support structure to support WBL. In creating regional teams, each region has a Kansas State Department of Education (KSDE) consultant to provide materials and activities for WBL, a community college partner to support academics, and one mediator from the local workforce development board that connects local businesses to schools. As of the 2022–2023 school year, 277 schools were supported by these regional teams. In total, 23,000 students have participated (Casalapsi et al., 2025, p. 18).

The report cites that Kansas's approach was successful because of the strong partnerships created, the use of key data to inform their work, and the documentation of information helped to analyze it. Students had to complete an individual plan of study (IPS). This plan allowed students to explore career interests, set goals for their high school career and beyond, understand a road map to achieving their goals, and identify classes and WBL opportunities for the student (Kansas State Department of Education, n.d.). The IPS is developed by the student, school counselor, teachers, and parents. This comprehensive approach allows for individualized attention to the student.

Overall, the strong partnerships created, the individualized plan for student learning, and multiple systems of support led to strong WBL experiences for students. The study discusses the logistical challenges of completing a lot of paperwork, high-quality training for all members involved, and ensuring students are in well-matched placements. At the core of the program that Kansas created is the holistic support system that addresses the various needs of WBL. Consider how you can help support students with creating a road map to their future, cultivate strong partnerships, and be open to learning more about WBL.

As discussed in earlier chapters, there are numerous programs to help document hours, find lesson plans for WBL and employability skills, and learn about WBL. Start with your school's resources first. Talk to your coordinators and focus on your students before looking outside. Understand what types of resources you are looking for.

## Comprehensive Local Needs Assessment

If schools are receiving Perkins V, known as the Strengthening Career and Technical Education for 21st Century Act, they need to conduct a comprehensive local needs assessment (CLNA) to be eligible to receive funding (ACTE, 2025). The purpose of the CLNA is to provide opportunities to reflect on the current programs, better align needs to the school, and collaborate with a wide variety of stakeholders to improve programming. As a CTE teacher, you might be asked to sit on a CLNA committee. Each committee needs to have CTE program representatives, like administrators, teachers, guidance professionals, parents, students, representatives from businesses, and representatives for special populations. If you serve on a committee, it is important to be open and honest as you discuss. It is important to base the conversation and decisions on the data. The data is used to identify gaps and inform program improvement. Be prepared to advocate for the needs of students and the opportunities they can benefit from. Know your data, strengths, and weaknesses before the meeting. Typically, an agenda is sent out before reviewing the information. Comprehensive Local Needs Assessment

If schools are receiving Perkins V, known as the Strengthening Career and Technical Education for 21st Century Act, they need to conduct a CLNA to be eligible to receive funding (ACTE, 2025). The purpose of the CLNA is to provide opportunities to reflect on the current programs, better align needs to the school, and collaborate with a wide variety of stakeholders to improve programming. As a CTE teacher, you might be asked to sit on a CLNA committee. Each committee needs to have CTE program representatives, like administrators, teachers, guidance professionals, parents, students, representatives from businesses, and representatives for special populations. If you serve on a committee, it is important to be open and honest as you discuss. It is important to base the conversation and decisions on the data. The data is used to identify gaps and inform program improvement. Be prepared to advocate for the needs of students and the opportunities they can benefit from. Know your data, strengths, and weaknesses before the meeting. Typically, an agenda is sent out before reviewing the information. CLNA can truly help shape school districts and improve CTE for the students.

## School Counselor Spotlight

Forging a strong partnership with school counselors is key to empowering CTE students for long-term success, as exemplified by Jason Finley at the Hartford Area Career and Technology Center. Jason has served in various roles that have shaped his philosophy of education and how he approaches being a school counselor. He has served as a Career Services Coordinator, Director of Career Education and Flexible Pathways, and Associate Principal.

Jason wants CTE teachers to know the importance of working with the school counselors and what strategies they can use. In Jason's school, they also have a full-time and share-time model. Since share-time teachers only see their students for two hours plus each day, they sometimes feel limited in their time with students attending assemblies and time with the school counselor, as a barrier to ensuring students learn all their technical skills. While Jason knows how important all those skills are to learn, he also advocates for ensuring students know how they can continue to level up their skills and be successful in the real world.

Have students, regardless of full-time or share-time, attend career fairs. He encourages CTE teachers to work with their school counselors to help prepare them for the career fair. He has students look at the various businesses attending the career fair and pick 2–3 they must see. Students then pick questions from a question bank to ask the employer. These questions range from asking about the culture of the company to asking about perks like paying for further education. Jason shared a compelling story illustrating how external voices can sometimes resonate more powerfully than even a trusted counselor's advice. Her entire family was in the field, and she couldn't wait to get started. She didn't see a point in pursuing more education. At a career fair all students attended, she talked to an employer about her future, who actually recommended continuing education in the field she was interested in. While Jason had told her to keep her options open and just explore post-secondary, she had her mind made up. Sometimes, the outside business, person, or organization can have a stronger impact on students.

When students attend a career fair and need to preplan, they learn valuable skills they can use in the future to navigate the changing job market. Jason poses good questions for CTE teachers to consider:

- ♦ Can students identify areas and opportunities in their career field of interest where they have strong aptitudes?
- ♦ Can students demonstrate knowledge and skills to map out their future careers independently?

For many students, the support and knowledge needed to discuss post-secondary plans with their families are simply not there. The career fair is just the beginning. After the event, it's essential to spend time with students discussing their key takeaways and "aha" moments. This follow-up session signals the importance of the fair and provides an opportunity to help students set concrete, actionable next steps. You can help them identify which companies or colleges to research further, whom to contact for more information, or what courses to consider taking to align with their new interests.

Another method Jason knows many teachers incorporate is guest speakers. He wants students to engage with them. He urges teachers to plan and prepare for them. Ask guest speakers to talk about their journey and day-to-day responsibilities. Make sure students prepare questions.

In trying to work with teachers, he spends time in the hallways, catching teachers between classes. These hallway conversations are an entry point to collaboration. He can learn what teachers are doing in the classroom and propose different ways to partner. His vision for the future of school counseling and CTE is to help students plan for the future better and really "level up" their skills. When Jason talks about students needing to "level up" their skills, he's challenging this kind of thinking. For that student heading into construction, "leveling up" isn't just about getting a job after high school; it's about understanding the pathways for advancement. It means recognizing that while an entry-level position is a great start, certifications in specific machinery operation, becoming a licensed journeyman, or even pursuing a degree in construction management are all ways to significantly increase earning potential, job security, and leadership opportunities within the trades. He wants students to see that businesses often pay for these exact "level up" opportunities, so they're not just getting a job, they're building a sustainable, thriving career. He wants to work with CTE teachers to help students break cycles of poverty and trauma and energize students to take control of their futures. He has seen too many students sitting in presentations where students are asking zero questions and just shutting the door on post-secondary options. He knows the value of different credentials, certifications, and degrees. He also knows many businesses in the trades will pay for their employees to continue their education.

While Jason isn't a WBL coordinator, he demonstrates how important all school members are in working with our students. Being able to prepare students to leave the support system of high school and enter the workforce is the core of a CTE program. As you think about designing your WBL, think about it as a sequential program that builds skills each year for students.

Your commitment to WBL directly shapes the future workforce and ignites the potential in every student you have. Being able to carefully plan meaningful experiences starting from the minute students enter your program to graduation is not an easy feat. However, by intentionally building robust partnerships with businesses, designing compelling and standards-aligned lessons, and providing a rich tapestry of varied experiences, you are embodying the very core of transformative WBL. This dedication cultivates not just skilled professionals but resilient, confident individuals ready to navigate the complexities of the real world. Embrace the ongoing challenge and profound reward of this work; your efforts are truly building bridges from the classroom to fulfilling careers.

 **Recommended Reading**

- *Transformational Work-Based Learning: Leading Exceptional Internship Programs* by Kristy Volesky.
- *Motivating Students Who Don't Care: Proven Strategies to Engage All Learners* by Allen N. Mendler.

 **Discussion Questions**

- How can we move WBL beyond simply "exposure" to true "engagement" and "experience" for all students?
- For your industry, what "big picture" aspects or "hidden realities" do you hope students would discover through an authentic WBL experience? How might this shape their career aspirations?
- Who can you partner with at school to design career-ready lessons with?
- Where do you want your students to be in 5 or 10 years?
- How do we effectively measure the "return on investment" of WBL for students (e.g., skill development, career clarity, post-secondary success)?

# References

ACTE. (2025, February). *Perkins 101: Comprehensive Local Needs Assessment.* acteonline.org. www.acteonline.org/wp-content/uploads/2025/03/ACTE-Perkins101-CLNA-Feb2025

Casalapsi, D., Graziano, L., & Foster, K. R. (2025, February 19). *Making It Work: Ten Stories of Promise and Progress in High School Work-based Learning.* Bellwether. https://bellwether.org/publications/making-it-work/

Kansas State Department of Education. (n.d.). *Individual Plans of Study (IPS) – Student.* KSDE. Retrieved July 21, 2025. www.ksde.gov/Agency/Division-of-Learning-Services/Career-Standards-and-Assessment-Services/Content-Area-F-L/Individual-Plans-of-Study-IPS-Student

Kansas Work-Based Learning: Personalized Learning Plan Guidance Document. (2019, July 31). KSDE. Retrieved July 20, 2025. www.ksde.gov/Portals/0/CSAS/CSAS%20Home/CTE%20Home/Kansas%20Work-Based%20Learning_Personalized%20Learning%20Plan.pdf

New Skills Ready Network. (n.d.). *Clearing the Path: Addressing Equity Blockers to Work-Based Learning in the New Skills Ready Network.* Education Strategy Group. https://edstrategy.org/wp-content/uploads/2023/08/Clearing-the-Path_New-Skills-Ready-Network.pdf

Princeton University. (n.d.). *Developing Your Elevator Pitch | Center for Career Development.* Center for Career Development. Retrieved July 22, 2025. https://careerdevelopment.princeton.edu/guides/networking/developing-your-elevator-pitch

Work-Based Learning (WBL) Tool Kit. (n.d.). Retrieved July 19, 2025. https://cte.ed.gov/wbltoolkit/index.html

World Economic Forum. (2025). *The Future of Jobs Report 2025.* https://www.weforum.org/publications/the-future-of-jobs-report-2025/digest/

# 5
# Grading and Assessments in CTE

During my first year, many teachers recommended using the check system in our gradebooks. Taking the advice of my colleagues, like any new teacher, I put a check in the gradebook if the students completed an assignment that was the equivalent to a class activity. The next day when I arrived at school, my inclusion teacher came flying into my room saying I gave everyone a 75. I said no, I gave everyone a check which equals a 100. She quickly explained check plus plus is 100, and I had to go fix all the grades before the students got upset. I was really confused who came up with this system. Why was there even a check plus and check plus plus? When I later talked to my mentor about my grading mistake, she questioned my grading practices. What did giving a 100 or a check plus plus tell my students about their work? I wanted to reward students for completing the work, but it also showed students they could hand in anything and would receive a good grade. It took me many discussions later to grapple with big grading questions like should I be grading on completion? What does excellent work look like in my classroom? How do students know how they are doing? What is the purpose of a grade? What does an "A" mean?

Grading and assessment is a topic that is often dreaded by students and even teachers. There are many misconceptions, deep rooted beliefs, and emotions around grades. For some students, good grades and report cards mean rewards from parents or a punishment from parents. Good grades are also synonymous with getting into a good college or being eligible for a scholarship. At a foundational level, good grades are often seen as being smart. However, grades fail to really communicate the entire picture of a student. It fails to recognize how hard a student worked on an assignment, what outside factors impacted a student learning during the time, or how responsible that student was.

Grades are a tool to communicate how well a student has mastered the content in the class. They are used as a way to indicate student strengths and weaknesses, inform parents about student learning, determine academic achievement, and level students. Grades are assigned based on the various assessments a student takes through a defined period of time. Schools assign marking periods or semesters that are a set amount of time. Students earn a grade during that time based on the set of assignments given by the teacher. Careful planning and thought surrounding grades and assignment for the marking period or semester is critical. Assignments and grades are too often an afterthought by teachers due to a lack of planning time.

In my own grading journey, I realized I have to really understand what my standards are in order to assess my students. I grappled with the idea that students won't receive grades in their future careers, but they will receive performance evaluations, reviews on their business, and recommendations. While they may not earn an A, the evaluations of the real world are impactful of a successful career. When students are in school, grades are a way for students to understand their mastery of the standards in each subject. Grades are then a communication tool. As you read this chapter on grading and assessment, think about your own beliefs and challenge your thinking. Grading is such a complex topic, and exploring your own beliefs and barriers will empower you as a teacher.

Many schools use the traditional grading system of 0–100 or A–F letter grades. The single grade is made from tests, quizzes, homework, and projects. Teachers will usually assign certain percentages to the various categories within the gradebook. Some schools will mandate the categories or allow teachers to choose as a department. Here are some various categories that are offered traditionally and for CTE. Schools and teachers will weigh each category differently based on their own beliefs and focus.

| Traditional categories | CTE categories |
|---|---|
| Tests | Learning activities |
| Quizzes | Authentic assessments |
| Homework | Career-ready practices |
| Projects | |
| Participation | Other categories: |
| | Performance-based |
| Or | Theory |
| | Skills-based |
| Formative | |
| Summative | |

There are several issues that arise with the traditional grading system used in schools. The grading conversation is also a large one that cannot be covered in this one chapter. First, grades are often used as behavior management. Teachers often take points off for handing in work late, not participating, or misbehaving. In the traditional grading category, participation, teachers can set arbitrary rules for students to learn. This might include "participates a certain amount of time", or "not following classroom rules", or "disrupts others". Next, grades are used as a motivation tool for students to complete work. Teachers will sprinkle extra points for completing certain tasks. Even more damaging, teachers might give a student a zero for not handing in an assignment. If the teacher fails to let the student resubmit, it can mean failure for the student. Teachers might also say "if you complete this assignment, you will get an A". Motivating students with grades contributes to the culture of how we think and feel about grades. It reinforces that students earn grades based on behaviors instead of grades being a communication tool of what they have learned.

"Why did you give me an 86?". This question is one I've heard countless times from students. I follow up with the same sentence, "I didn't give you an 86, you earned this grade because … " and

I use specific language from the standard I was assessing. Our current grading system fails to give students and parents the information they need. It fosters a culture where students and parents just care about the letter or number they receive and lack the understanding of their learning. Students are eager to hear their grade but fail to look at the feedback or implement it next time. As teachers, we spend hours grading and providing detailed feedback that students ignore. What is the purpose if students don't use it? Students laser focus on the grade, completely ignoring the feedback attached to it. Once students see the grade, they either accept it and move on, still forgetting about the feedback because they feel they don't need to or they complain about the grade and blame the teacher. Next, there is a lack of inconsistency between teachers and grade levels. Each teacher, school, and grade level has their own beliefs about grading. An A earned at one school doesn't translate to an A at a different school. Teachers don't always use a rubric or grade objectively. They also don't always count the same assignments. Students learn how to play the game of school instead of learning how to be a lifelong learner. Where do we go from here and how does CTE use grades?

Fortunately, CTE teachers can implement strong grading practices because of the real-world connection. Since many CTE students work toward a real certification, grading students accurately and aligned to the industry is important and eliminates grading inflation. However, teachers sometimes fall into the trap of grading all assignments based on completion or failing to grade a student accurately. Grading for completion is giving students a 100, A, or other grade just for handing in an assignment. It actively disincentivizes students from trying hard, focusing on accuracy, or seeking to truly understand the material. If a perfect score is guaranteed just for submission, there's no motivation to put in genuine effort or to learn from mistakes. One common place this happens is with homework, the signed syllabus in the beginning of the year, returning tools, or practice assignments. We have this fear that students won't turn something in because it isn't attached to a grade. The most damaging consequence is the disconnect it creates in the learning narrative. For instance, consider a student who consistently receives a 100 for each homework assignment simply for turning it in, regardless of numerous errors. They might also receive completion grades for returning a signed syllabus or properly putting away tools. If this homework is only reviewed in class, and the teacher doesn't collect or assess the quality of the work (assuming students will self-correct), a few weeks later, this student might fail a unit test. The gradebook then tells a confusing story: a high average (inflated by completion grades) that directly contradicts the low summative assessment grade. Parents, accustomed to seeing high grades, become understandably confused, believing their student was performing well, only to be blindsided by a failing test score. This scenario profoundly misrepresents the student's true learning progress. Without specific, timely feedback on their errors, and without the incentive to apply that feedback for an improved grade, many students will simply repeat the same mistakes, solidifying misunderstandings rather than correcting them.

## Standards-Based Grading

As discussed in the earlier chapters, standards are important to guide student learning but also help provide an accurate grading system. Standards-based grading is a system that shifts the focus from grades to mastery of the standards. Standards-based grading is sometimes also referred to as competency-based grading or proficiency-based grading. The goal is to more accurately communicate what students have learned and what they can do (Link & Guskey, 2022). There are three core principles in standards-based grading that serve as its core values.

- ♦ Grades serve as clear communication: Grades convey a student's present level of learning and their progress toward mastering specific standards.
- ♦ Homework is ungraded practice: Homework serves as an opportunity for low-stakes practice and feedback, not for point accumulation. Students are able to take risks and learn from mistakes without penalizing their overall grade.

♦ Multiple opportunities for mastery: Students are given several chances to demonstrate their understanding and improve their performance. This reflects that learning is a process, not a single event (Townsley & Wear, 2020, p. 8).

Standards-based grading provides more information and a clearer picture of what students know and what they can do. When grades are aligned to standards, it takes the guesswork out of what is important to learn and what needs to be done to meet the expectations (Link & Guskey, 2022). Typically standards-based grading involves assigning a score of 1–4 that reflects mastery of the standard (Townsley & Wear, 2020, p. 28). Mastery is communicated, typically through a rubric that clearly defines the levels of performance. A score of "4" would mean exceeding/mastery, meaning the student demonstrates a deep understanding and can apply the skill consistently and may be able to teach others. A score of "3" would mean meeting/proficient, meaning the student demonstrates a solid understanding of the standard. The scale would continue to go down where "1" would demonstrate a student has minimal or no understanding of the standard.

This standard is from the NJ CTE teaching and training pathway: "Employ knowledge of learning and developmental theory to describe individual learners" (New Jersey Department of Education, 2025).

In looking at this standard, there is a lot of background content students need to be introduced to before mastering this standard. I will focus on teaching students about how learning happens, exploring what motivates learners, different learning theories before focusing on how individuals change and diving into development. Students will need to recall the information and apply it in a meaningful way. Students would have several opportunities to demonstrate their knowledge, receive feedback, and make adjustments to master their own learning. Thus, this one single line might equate to a month long unit in my classroom. I typically will make a list of different practice assignments that students engage in for feedback in mastering this standard. The practice assignments are not just busy work. They serve as diagnostic checkpoints to gauge where students are struggling and excelling. Each assignment builds on their learning and ultimately, for success on the summative assessment.

For schools to take on complete standards-based grading, all stakeholders would need to be involved in planning. While you are not in a position to change your school's official grading system, you can implement some principles of standards-based grading to make your grades an accurate reflection of student learning and clearly communicate to students.

| Traditional grading (0–100) system | Standards-based infusion |
| --- | --- |
| ♦ Work has a purpose but might lack connection to the standard<br>♦ Homework/class activities are graded for correctness or completion<br>♦ Limited opportunities for students to revise work<br>♦ Assignments are penalized for late work | ♦ Clear learning targets for work are provided<br>♦ Homework/class activities are ungraded and serve as a tool for feedback and practice<br>♦ Multiple opportunities for students to demonstrate mastery<br>♦ Behaviors and work completion are graded separately |

There is no single grading system that is perfect and attitudes on grade remain emotional for teachers, parents, and students. As you consider your own practices in grading, think about how you can infuse strong practices to clearly communicate student learning.

## Learning Targets

It is obvious to say that in standards-based grading, the standards are the main focus but how do we accomplish this? In Myron Dueck's *Giving Students a Say,* he urges to share educational theory and terminology with students (Dueck, 2021, p. 22). Students should be taught how to create learning targets.

Learning targets are student-friendly statements that are made based on the learning standards and include verbs and nouns. Learning targets lead to creating clear assessment criteria and help students have a strong understanding of their learning (Townsley & Wear, 2020, p. 23).

| NJ Learning Standard | Learning target |
|---|---|
| "Employ knowledge of learning and developmental theory to describe individual learners" (New Jersey Department of Education, 2025) | I will be able to apply what I've learned about different learning styles and developmental stages to better understand the needs of individual learners |

It seems simple to transform the language into student-friendly targets. The target can serve as a guide for students and helps infuse the language into their learning. Learning scales are a skill progression that includes the learning target (Townsley & Wear, 2020, p. 33). Here is a learning scale using the same NJ Learning Standard we've been discussing, built with positive "I can" statements that put the student in charge of their own learning:

1. I am beginning to recognize that different people learn and develop in unique ways.
2. I can recognize different learning theories and define key terms.
3. I can apply my knowledge of learning and developmental theories to describe and explain a learner's actions and motivations.
4. I can accurately use multiple learning and developmental theories to analyze a learner's behavior and create a strategy to help them.

By making the expectations transparent, a teacher can have a conversation with a student that moves beyond a simple grade and focuses instead on where they are in their learning journey. This clarity also guides your instruction. For instance, if you observe many students operating at a "Level 2", you know you need to adjust your teaching to provide more scaffolded practice in applying the theories.

In improving transparency and aligning grades better, Myron Dueck encourages teachers to use a student-friendly unit plan. This is a simple yet impactful strategy that takes the teacher's plan for learning and translates it into a clear, concise roadmap that students can follow. A student-friendly unit plan effectively demystifies the learning process by putting all the essential information in one place. It typically includes:

- Learning Targets
  The learning targets are listed to answer the question "what do I need to know and what can I demonstrate?" (Dueck, 2014, p. 79). They are listed in a progression order so students can visualize the learning.
- Practice Activities
  A list of all assignments and activities that students will engage in during the unit is provided. I like including this, so students know exactly where the unit is going and the work expected of them. I also list if the assignment will be graded or ungraded.
- Summative Assessments
  Since summative assessments are the driver of the learning to assess the standard, including this is paramount.

On the unit plan, you can have students track their scores, set goals, and reflect on their learning. Students become active participants in their own learning, able to self-assess their progress, ask targeted questions, and take ownership of their journey toward mastery. This single tool brings all the principles of standards-based grading together, transforming abstract standards into a clear, achievable path for every student (Dueck, 2014, p. 81).

## Strategies for Getting Students to Complete Work

Why are we doing this? A common question that despite my best communication efforts, I receive from students. Students want to know why and they want to care about the work. In a social media group with other CTE teachers, hundreds of people commented about the lack of care students have for their grades, themselves, and their learning. If students do not have their needs being met on a personal level, it will be a huge challenge to get them to care about the project in front of them. For these students, they need extra time, attention, and someone in their corner that doesn't write them off or give up. The following strategies are for the majority of students in the classroom. Providing purposeful assignments will be the biggest factor in motivating students to complete the work. For example, in a culinary class, students learn different knife skills using a variety of foods which ultimately build in plating a dish. Students will have multiple opportunities to practice the knife skills. The culminating task is cutting vegetables and meat then cooking it before serving it to a panel teacher and administrators. In this task, students will practice for hours cutting and trying different techniques. The motivation is high because their skill is going to be displayed and evaluated by multiple people. What I found difficult in achieving are the smaller theory assignments that build to the culminating activity.

**Honest Communication**

Being able to communicate effectively with students about the purpose of their assignment is paramount. I wanted students to listen to a 10 minute podcast and record their thoughts on the podcast. One student raised their hand and said "what's the point in doing this?". All eyes in the classroom were one me. I took a deep breath and simply explained the skill of active listening and evaluating a podcast was going to lead us into our next project. As I braced for a response filled with attitude, she replied with "okay". This quick conversation reminded me that students just want to have control too and know why things need to be done. Explain to students how things build on one another. It seems simple but often forgotten by teachers. The line "because I said so" is dated and fails our students each time we say it. While students need to be respectful and listen to what we say, this line doesn't accomplish anything. Creating a chart, outline, or simple table of the various assignments and their connection to learning serves as a communication tool. It also enhances the purpose of each assignment.

It is also important to change your vocabulary. Words, like assigning a grade, have meaning and send signals to the students. Instead of homework, I say "learning activity". This communicates the assignment is key to their learning and provides opportunity to practice important skills or concepts. Homework, unfortunately, has developed a negative connotation.

**Checkpoints**

Providing students with deadlines and checkpoints while working on a large project gives direction and eliminate students having an incomplete project by the due date. Checkpoints help break up a project for students who struggle with breaking down an assignment. It can also teach students how to effectively break up an assignment. As students become more familiar with projects and procedures, challenge students to create their own checkpoints for a project.

For each checkpoint, I use it as a form of communication and not a punitive grade. In my gradebook computer system, I am to enter non-graded assignments and weigh assignments at zero. By entering it into my school's main communication tool, it allows students and parents to theoretically be in the know. I also will talk to the student in class and comment on our learning management system. After two or three checkpoints, I will email the student and copy the parents. This consistent documentation is crucial; it demonstrates that we've provided multiple opportunities for students to complete their work and receive support. While it might sometimes feel like you're "chasing" a student, we must ask ourselves: Why wouldn't we afford every student every possible opportunity and layer of support to succeed and learn? As we also have discussed, students are still developing. The proactive intervention acts as an early warning system for students who might be struggling or failing behind before it significantly impacts their summative grade. It also builds student self-regulation. Students start to learn how to monitor their own work habits and advocate for help when they need while preparing them for the demands of the workplace

**Skills Sheet**
Similar to a checklist for completing assignments, at the start of each unit or marking period, develop a task sheet aligned with the essential skills for that learning period. This resource enables students to engage in self-directed practice during workshop time, fostering independent learning. It can serve as a tool for students to own their learning. This sheet can be used as a formative assessment tool. A quick glance can tell the teacher which students are moving quickly and which may need individualized support.

**Meaningful Workshop Time**
When students engage in meaningful projects, it should include student choice. Since students will be focusing on the same standard, providing independent time or workshop time is key. Giving students the space to grapple with standards, work on assignments at their own pace reinforces accountability and grows student independence. Avoid having students have no plan or the class time to figure it out themselves. Students need to be taught how to use their independent time wisely. Purposeful workshop time helps the students own their work, make mistakes and learn from them, learn from each other, and communicate with the teacher. At the start of the class, have students set a goal for the time. During the workshop time, have a plan. You can have students sign up for conferences with you or schedule mini-workshops that are small group instruction. This can be a time to help pull students that need extra instruction on a specific skill or enhance a specific skill. At the end of the workshop, have students note their progress.

**Feedback**
The goal of feedback is not just to correct, but to guide students toward mastery, and it doesn't always have to be formal, written, and tied to a grade. It can be a quick verbal

check-in, a peer-to-peer critique during a workshop, or a simple comment on a draft.

To ensure students actively engage with feedback, some educators leverage the grade itself. For example, they may provide detailed feedback on an assignment but delay posting the final grade until students confirm they have reviewed the comments and made revisions. This method prompts a more active engagement with the critique. Another highly effective strategy is to design a sequence of assignments where each new task intentionally builds on the previous one. In this structured approach, students must apply the feedback from an earlier assignment to successfully complete the next, transforming feedback from a suggestion into a necessary tool for their own progress and learning.

**Peer Review**

When students are working on projects, implementing purposeful peer review can help students receive feedback but also practice giving feedback. Peer review is when students give feedback to each other on their work. Some downfalls about peer review are students lack the expertise to give meaningful feedback, students are nervous about giving a critique, or students don't give enough feedback. Peer review can provide students with the tools they need to be successful. A traditional peer review involves two students swapping projects to give feedback on. Some teachers use a two stars and one wish method. Students write down two things they felt were strong about a project and one thing that could be improved. This method is a start to students giving feedback but often comes out superficial. Students will comment "I like the colors you used" or "The idea was creative".

One strategy to allow students to get more feedback and give more feedback is a gallery walk with purpose. Each student is assigned one specific component to give feedback on. Students pass the project to each student and give feedback or walk around to each project. This strategy will work with most projects. What works about this method is a student is only responsible for one component on the rubric. For example, one student just gives feedback on a professional, another student gives feedback on content, and the list goes on.

## Tips and Advice

Grading in a timely manner and reporting the grades to the grading system for students and parents to see are important. Creating a schedule to grade can prevent blinding students and parents. After a major assignment is due, be sure to enter "missing" into the gradebook so parents and students can be aware and it doesn't surprise students at the end of the marking period. Be careful to not assign assessments near the end of the marking period or semester. Students often have assignments piling up from all subjects around the same time.

## Career-Ready Practices

Since grades are meant to be a tool for communicating about a student's mastery of standards, career-ready practices offer a way to measure student accountability and communicate that to students. Career-ready practices provide a framework that focuses on what it means to be successful in a career. The framework includes 12 different standards that focus on acting responsible, applying skills, communication clearly, demonstrating creativity, and using critical thinking (Advance CTE, 2023). Some schools may also call these employability skills.

Career-ready practices grades can be implemented to give feedback to students and penalize them for late work. It provides more meaning than taking a certain amount of points from an assessment. Using a rubric, this grade can be assigned once every two weeks, once a week, and once a month depending on how often the program meets. A tip while implementing career-ready practice grades is to have a clipboard with student names or your laptop up during class to capture student actions in the moment. For example, during class if a student participates you can add this or if a student is playing a game on the computer. Writing the actions down in the moment leads to more informative career-ready practices instead of trying to remember after class.

Here is an example of one way to write down the actions in the moment. Some teachers have developed a key so they use symbols or check marks to track the student behavior.

| Student name | 9/4 | 9/5 | 9/6 | 9/7 | 9/8 |
|---|---|---|---|---|---|
| Student A | On phone participated | | Participated | Taught someone else | |
| Student B | | Forgot uniform | Playing games on phone | | |

Depending on the grading system, communicating feedback while in process is important. Being able to input this information daily allows students to have almost instant feedback. Avoid feeling pressure to have something each day for students. It is important to truly capture every single action a student does. It is also important to have high expectations for students. Certain behaviors are expected and students should not be rewarded with a higher grade for simply following rules. For example, handing things on time earns students a "meeting expectation" grade but does not exceed expectations.

The first few weeks of school are important for setting expectations for grades and career-ready practices. During the few days of school, discussing and reviewing career-ready practices allows students to be vigilant about their expectations in the class. One activity that works well in using student voice and setting clear expectations is the use of career-ready task cards. First, give students a copy of the CRP rubric you will use in class. Have students highlight key words that stick out to them. Students can even brainstorm a checklist that can be used in each class. Next, give students the task cards to categorize. The task cards have different student behaviors on them, one behavior for each card. The behaviors range from exceeding expectations to no effort from the students. Putting different behaviors that teachers see each day in their class creates an open conversation about the expectations. It also provides key insight from students to better understand their thinking and can avoid miscommunications. An example card says "students use their cell phones after all their work is complete". Many students think this action is okay, but as a teacher, the expectation may be different. Leave one care blank to have students create a behavior to add. Students in their groups will categorize the card according to the rubric. When students are finished, have each group present the created behavior card and share what card led to the most discussion. There are certain cards as the teacher I bring up to discuss. This includes what to do in certain situations during work-based learning, cell phone use, and group work. Consider what is important to your classroom flow. After discussing CRPs, create a class contract where students contribute behaviors they need to see in the classroom to be successful. At the end of the marking period or semester, have students reflect on their career-ready practices. Students can set new goals based on their reflection for the next marking period.

## Common Misconceptions

### Late Work

Students are often self-proclaimed procrastinators, and there is much controversy around late work policies. Taking points away from an assignment is supposed to show accountability and give a consequence to students handing in an assignment late. Grades should reflect how students have mastered a standard. So, where does late work fit into the grade? Why do students' hand in work late? Should you take late points off the assignment? In the "real world", showing up late to a client's house for a plumbing job could make you lose your client. Handing in a proposal late could mean missing grant money or an opportunity at all. How can we translate this concept to students? Simple career-ready practices like handing in work on time can be the difference between you and another company. Consider the lessons you want your students to learn and how meaningful a grade is.

While deducting points for late submissions might aim to deter future tardiness, it obscures the actual quality of the work. A student who produces an "A" caliber plumbing project, earning a 90, could see their grade artificially lowered to an 80 due to lateness. This practice diminishes the grade's ability to accurately reflect their mastery of the material. Some students will habitually turn assignments in late regardless of points being taken off. Thus, the late system and grades will not deter students or "teach them the lesson". It only continues to fail students.

If you have an employability grade or career-ready practice grade, consider reflecting that grade instead of the project. More importantly, a conversation with the student often uncovers the real issue of why the assignment was late. If you use other strategies like checkpoints throughout the project, conferencing, and project checklist, it significantly decreases late work. It also acts as an early warning system if a student is going to hand in the project late.

I've had students who habitually handed in assignments late. It seemed no matter how many checkpoints, conferences, emails to parents, or checklists I gave the student, at the final hour, they always had an excuse. Typically, this is a larger problem that happens outside just my class. I speak with the school counselor about what is going on. Unfortunately, some students just need time to grow. However, don't give up hope and celebrate their small wins. When they do complete a check point, praise them! The constant positive encouragement will eventually have large pay offs.

**Extra Credit**
Extra credit is usually an optional "extra" thing a student can do to earn points to improve a grade. Some examples of extra credit include extra test questions at the end of a test, a worksheet students can complete, or an additional project. Extra credit is meant to help students who need the extra point. However, there is a case against extra credit. Students are expected to complete all the work assigned during the marking period. If grades are truly meant to reflect their mastery of the

standard, then extra credit inflates their grade. Often, students might focus on completing the extra credit instead of focusing on improving their work. Extra credit is often completed by the students that are already overachieving and mastering concepts in a class.

If you do assign extra credit or have an extra credit question, relate it to content. It might be fun to add a personal question like "Name Ms. Shane's favorite instructional strategy", but this question isn't fair or relates to the learning standards. Never make an extra credit assignment about another student. For example, "Write a letter to Samantha about why she is a good student". Even if the students all love Samantha, it can metaphorically open a can of worms. Students should never be singled out. Even further, other students shouldn't be forced to write about another student. Be intentional about the extra credit you assign. Focus on the purpose and how it serves your students.

## Reassessments

Should I allow reassessments and how do I grade it? Grades are often assigned and forgotten about once they enter the gradebook. Similar to completing a job, once the job is done and the customer is happy, you move on to the next job. Reassessments allow students to learn from their mistakes, teaching them resilience and grit. Students can refine their efforts, which is how most professionals learn on the job. Reassessments allow students to retake an assessment to demonstrate mastery and learning. This can look like giving a new test to a student, fixing mistakes on an assessment, or a completely different assessment. The idea of reassessment is well-intended but sometimes hard to navigate with the constraints of a marking period. First, you need to consider if you will allow reassessments or not. If the answer is yes, think about your system for implementing reassessments.

Students should build in classroom time for reteaching before students reassess. This also doesn't mean students should be staying after school to relearn. Students can be pulled for small group instruction, guided practice during workshop time, or individual instruction (Townsley & Wear, 2020, p. 87). To avoid all students constantly making up all their assessments, some teachers have created reassessment forms that students complete if they want to make up a test. Students will explain why they want to take a reassessment and when. Teachers then have the power to deny the student's request and shouldn't have an open door policy for reassessments. A timeline for allowing a reassessment should be established since content tends to move fast and marking period dates matter. This might look like a one or two week timeframe. Teachers also don't have to force students to reassess. Some students will not want to redo a test. Reassessments can help with promoting fairness and equity. Like us, students do have "off" days" or just simply need a little more time with a concept.

When grading a test that is a reassessment, teachers have a few different approaches. First, the teacher might fully replace the original grade with the reassessment. Another option is averaging the grade from the original test with the reassessment. Teachers also have students fix mistakes on tests for partial credit. This encourages students to review their work and understand their errors without making up a new test. Clearly communicate which option you might use to students if you allow reassessments. Be specific about what reassessments will look like and how they are being graded. Being proactive in reinforcing that reassessments are not a bailout but an opportunity to demonstrate continued learning.

## Homework

Homework serves as a way to strengthen skills learned during class. It also serves as a major pain point for teenagers that have after school clubs or sports, long commutes, family obligations, jobs, tutoring, and/or other after school commitments that prevent students from completing homework. John Hattie's meta-analysis suggests the positive influence homework has on high school learners (Hattie, 2023, p. 20). Some schools may have a school-wide policy on homework for students; be sure to familiarize yourself with the policy. Homework needs to be purposeful in providing feedback for learning. Best practice also cites that homework should be ungraded, but when teachers give feedback on homework, it increases students completing their homework and improves student outcomes (Townsley & Wear, 2020, p. 54). We have the responsibility to make homework meaningful if we plan on assigning it. If homework is going to be busy work that you don't use in the next class, think about forgetting it. Having students complete practice problems to reinforce a skill can be a good exercise but try implementing that in class the next day as the warm up. Instead, have students watch a video, interview a parent, or explore a new resource. Think about homework as an opportunity to extend learning, foster curiosity, or prepare students for the next lesson in an engaging way. By shifting our approach to homework, we can transform it from a compliance task into a genuine learning opportunity that fosters deeper understanding, critical thinking, and engagement.

**Grading Group Work**

How many times have you worked as part of a team and someone didn't pull their weight? How often has someone received credit for all your hard work? This feeling is often replicated when we grade group work. As discussed in Chapter 2, group work is a beneficial strategy that encourages students to collaborate and engage with one another. Grading a group project might come with some challenges. The strategies outlined in Chapter 2 like a group contract and assigned roles will be proactive in ensuring students receive a fair grade.

If you plan on grading group work, be sure to be explicit in how you are grading students. If students are assigned roles, how is each role being graded? You might want to consider a rubric for each role. Grades are a measurement of how students are mastering the standards. If each group member receives the same grade, how can you ensure each student is proficient in that standard? If you plan on assigning the same grade to each student, have students complete a detailed list of parts of the project they completed. Have a plan in place if students complain or you observe students not completing work. Make students complete a contract and hold them to the contract.

## Assessments

A few months ago, I had a pipe start leaking through my ceiling. I called a plumber to come assess the issue which he quickly found, made a recommendation, and was hired. The term assessment is often a misconception in education. It is often thought of as a formal test with multiple choice questions that measures the understanding of a unit or chapter. Teachers are constantly taking in data informally or formally about their students. When considering assessments, there are two main types. Formative assessments inform instruction and guide instructional decisions to improve student learning. Summative assessments are "intentional and purposely designed to provide reliable, individual achievement and they come at the end of an intentional cycle" (Rinkema & Williams, 2018, p. 58). Replacing the pipe in my leaking ceiling can be thought of as a summative assessment. The purpose of a summative assessment is to serve as a final measurement to assess student learning and mastery of the standards. Typically, students move to a new unit after the completion of the summative. Some examples of summative assessment are traditional tests, projects, practical assessments, essays, and presentations. When designing a summative assessment, consider the task and what the best way to measure learning and demonstrate mastery of the standards. Whichever type of summative assessment you chose, you want to be intentional on the design and implementation.

Assessments drive the learning and shouldn't be an afterthought. Teachers should begin planning a unit with the end of unit assessment in mind. Formative assessments are benchmarks for students as they work toward the summative assessment. These types of assessments are ongoing and provide feedback to students throughout a unit and provide feedback to the teacher. Examples of formative assessments are exit tickets, homework, questions, teacher observations, and/or practice problems (O'Connor, 2017, p. 123). Formative assessments aren't always a formal assignment; they are an opportunity to provide feedback and check for understanding. Simply engaging students in questioning to understand their thinking counts as a formative assessment. Another example is students giving a quick rating on their confidence level or thumbs up/down for understanding. Research shows that the shorter the time interval between eliciting evidence and using it to improve, the bigger the likely impact on learning (Wiliam & Leahy, 2015, p. 9). Formative assessments are meant to inform that if there is too much time between students completing the assignment and receiving feedback, it might become meaningless to their learning.

Since formative assessments provide feedback on student learning, there are many arguments if formative assessments should be graded or ungraded. Since students are still learning the concept, formative assessments serve as feedback. However, in school systems, we need grades to fill our gradebooks. Follow your school's protocol for formative grades. But consider what assignments you choose to grade. Formative assessments are a great opportunity for students to interact with the learning, uncover misconceptions, and take risks. A CTE teacher uses formative assessments constantly, often without even consciously labeling them as such, because their environment is so hands-on and performance-based. For example, when introducing a new tool, you provide time for students to practice using the tool. This could include holding it, balancing it, pressing buttons or levers, and miming the motions required for its safe and effective operation. You observe students and comment on their grip, technique, and watch them explore. It gives you data on how the students are doing. Then, you implement different activities for students to use the tool. While this chapter doesn't dive into specific formative assessments, go back to Chapter 2 to look at different formative assessments you can implement. When considering what formative assessments to use, be sure to have a clear view of learning.

Some schools will require students to take midterm/finals. These are benchmarks to test student learning for the course at the mid-point and end of year. These comprehensive assessments go beyond individual unit tests by evaluating a student's ability to recall and integrate concepts learned over an entire marking period or semester. They are often a requirement from the school or district to ensure a consistent measure of student learning. If your school does require midterms/finals, consider making these assessments performance-based or aligned to an industry-recognized credential. Further, CTE programs typically have an end of program assessment that typically leads to an industry-recognized credential. The previous chapter highlights the importance of industry-recognized credentials and how to implement them.

**Rubrics**

When we give students a number or letter grade on assignment, what does it really communicate? A rubric serves as a way to provide targeted feedback on assessments. According to Cornell University's Center for Teaching Innovation, "rubrics are a type of scoring guide that assesses and articulates specific components and expectations for an assignment" (Using Rubrics | Center for Teaching Innovation, n.d.). They help teachers consistently assess students and their assignments, give effective feedback, and clarify expectations. A quality rubric helps students better understand the learning expectation. Many websites and AI will help you create a rubric. Be sure to carefully read over what AI gives you to ensure your rubric accurately reflects the learning standard you hope to evaluate or give student feedback on. There are several types of rubrics that teachers can use and they each have different benefits. The two most common rubric types of holistic and analytic.

Analytic rubrics provide detailed feedback on each criterion. Each row of the rubric is scored. They provide specific feedback to students and link easily to the learning standards. A downside to analytic rubrics is they take a lot longer to create and score (Brookhart, 2023, p. 7). Holistic rubrics provide a score for all the criteria. The disadvantage of the holistic rubric is that the single overall score doesn't always communicate how to improve. There is one description that is applied for all the criterion points. Here are examples of holistic and analytic rubrics I've used in my classroom.

## Analytic Rubric

This rubric is taken from my podcast project.

| | Below expectations | Approaching expectations | Meets expectations | Above expectations |
|---|---|---|---|---|
| Content | Information is inaccurate, incomplete, or irrelevant to the chosen facet<br><br>No research or inaccurate research is used<br><br>Provides no applicable insights or suggestions for action | Provides some information about the impact, but lacks depth or clarity<br><br>Concepts lack research<br><br>Lacks clear takeaways or resources for applying knowledge | Analyzes the chosen facet with sufficient depth and insight<br><br>Concepts are mostly pulled from research<br><br>Offers some suggestions for action, but could be more specific and actionable | Clearly and comprehensively explores the specific facet of [Topic]'s impact on education<br><br>Concepts are cleverly pulled from research to showcase and defend the author's position<br><br>Concludes with practical takeaways and resources for applying knowledge to improve education |

*(Continued)*

|  | Below expectations | Approaching expectations | Meets expectations | Above expectations |
|---|---|---|---|---|
| Engagement | Presentation is dry, monotonous, or difficult to follow<br>Lacks engagement and captivation | Storytelling or presentation elements are somewhat lacking<br>Somewhat engaging and captivating | Episode maintains audience interest, but could be more dynamic<br>Mostly engaging and captivating | Has a strong hook that captivates the audience<br>Storytelling, interviews, and narration are engaging and captivating |
| Diversity of perspectives | Fails to present any diverse viewpoints or experiences<br>Lacks new ideas on the topic | Primarily focuses on one or two perspectives, lacking broader representation<br>Attempts a unique voice but is cliché or repetitive | Includes some diverse viewpoints, but could benefit from additional perspectives<br>Mostly unique voice on the topic | Features a variety of voices and perspectives from educators, historians, experts, and students<br>Offers a unique voice on the topic |
| Historical context | Episode ignores or misrepresents historical context | Historical context is briefly mentioned or inaccurate | Integrates historical context, but may lack detail or precision | Provides clear and accurate historical context for [Topic]'s impact on education |

| | | | |
|---|---|---|---|
| Overall quality | Episode is poorly organized, confusing, or uninformative<br>Grammar mistakes are significant<br>Three or more errors in sound<br>No transitions<br>Podcast is 3 or more minute under or over the time limit | Episode provides basic information but lacks depth or impact<br>Grammar mistakes are made and impact the podcast<br>Two–three errors in sound<br>Transitions are attempted, a lot of dead space<br>Podcast is 2 minutes under or over time limit | Episode is generally informative and interesting<br>Mostly correct grammar is used throughout the podcast<br>One–two errors in sound<br>Transitions are mostly smooth, some dead space<br>Podcast is 1 minute under or over time limit | Episode is informative, insightful, and thought-provoking<br>Correct grammar is used throughout the podcast<br>There are no errors in sound<br>Transitions are smooth and spaced correctly without noise; no dead space<br>Podcast is 10–15 minutes |

## Holistic Rubric

This rubric is taken from an assignment where my student engages with a current event in education and analyzes the impact on education.

| Score | Performance level description |
|---|---|
| Excellent | The analysis is exceptionally insightful, nuanced, and critical. It goes well beyond summarizing the article by synthesizing its core arguments and expertly connecting them to the unit's themes. The evaluation of best practices is sophisticated and well-supported, clearly articulating the significance of the information. The response to the guiding questions is thoughtful and demonstrates a deep understanding of the article's broader implications for education, and the personal viewpoint is clearly articulated. The final discussion questions are open-ended, creative, and highly likely to stimulate a productive and meaningful dialogue. |
| 3 – Proficient | The analysis is clear, well-structured, and focused. It successfully avoids excessive summary and identifies the main themes, making a solid and logical connection to the topics covered in the unit. The evaluation of the article's alignment with best practices is sound, and it identifies significant information with clear justification. The response thoughtfully addresses the guiding questions, and the implications for students and teachers are relevant and well-considered. The final two to three discussion questions are well-phrased, relevant, and designed to encourage further thought and discussion. |

| Score | Performance level description |
|---|---|
| 2 – Developing | The analysis is present but may be superficial, containing elements of summary rather than a clear focus on critical thought. It identifies some of the article's themes but struggles to make a deep or clear connection to the unit's topics. The evaluation of best practices is general, and the significance of the information is not fully explained. The response addresses the guiding questions but lacks depth or specific examples. The final discussion questions may be simple or not fully aligned with the core arguments of the article. |
| 1 – Beginning | The response is primarily a summary of the article, failing to provide substantial original analysis. It does not clearly identify the main themes, and little to no connection is made to the unit's topics. The evaluation of best practices and the significance of the information are either missing or incorrect. The guiding questions are not addressed, or the answers are vague and unsupported. |

When designing a rubric and creating descriptors, this question "What characteristics of student work would give evidence for students learning of the knowledge or skills specific in the standard?" (Brookhart, 2023, p. 26). It is important to ensure the description matches the learning standard language and target. Further, the two essential qualities of a good rubric are criteria that are linked to the learning standards and clear descriptions of performance (Brookhart, 2023, p. 10).

Rubrics bring clarity to the assignment and classroom but only when students engage with them. I've had countless times where students didn't look at the rubric until the day before the project was due or when I handed the rubric back with feedback.

The words "I didn't know I had to include … ", or "I don't even know what this means" would pain me. At first, I was frustrated with students; it was their job to read every word. But really, I was mad at myself. Students are still learning and growing; they need to be taught how to use a rubric effectively. Do not assume a previous teacher or another class has taught them. To avoid those painful sentences, spend time looking over the rubric with students. When students are completing a project, early in the process, I have students grade sample projects using the rubric. The sample projects vary in being quality. I want my students to not just recognize what meeting the standard looks like but common mistakes that students might make on the project. It also provides discussion around expectations. It is often during these moments I can see students thinking clearly. It allows students to take a deeper dive into the rubric, really understanding the language.

Students being able to see examples also help create their own vision. When showing students sample projects, make sure you remove the names and any identifying markers. If you can't, ask student permission. Put it in writing, this might look like an email to the student saying "Thank you for agreeing to let me use your project as a student exemplar". You want to avoid students taking pictures of the sample work, so students don't make fun of a project or completely copy it. You can also use AI to create a sample that would score lower on the standards.

To engage students further in their own assessment, consider adding a row of rubric that students can design. When this idea was first introduced to me, I didn't implement it well. I took my own rubric and simply added a blank row. I told students to add on criteria for the project, and I would grade it. As you might expect, I received a mixed bag of responses. My students were creating children's books for an elementary school. Some students really considered the project and purpose to create a meaningful rubric row, and other students added something very surface level. I knew I couldn't ignore what students wrote, but again, I was frustrated with myself. I failed to really understand the purpose and point of students being involved in co-creating the assessment.

Another misconception when using a rubric is using the rubric as assignment requirements or reaching a specific quantity. When rubrics include specific, quantity specific requirements, it becomes focused on the grade and "checking the box". For example, a less quality rubric may say "Includes six tools in the directions" or "Completed all the steps". They are vague, lack specificity, and are missing crucial details. The rubric and grading turn into assessing for compliance. Unfortunately, students will include the right number of tools but may lack the actual learning of the project. A tool to use is making your criteria performance-based.

## Cheating and Plagiarism

Unfortunately, students will cheat on tests and assignments. They will try to write formulas on their hand, sneak their cell phone, or even walk around the room to see answers. Students cheat because they didn't prepare enough, the stakes of doing poorly may be too high, they procrastinate, or they don't understand the content. The role of the teacher is to ensure students are prepared for assessments but also prevent cheating conditions. Students will look around the room while taking a test, discuss test questions with other students, and share answers. Be clear about the expectations during a test.

To create optimal testing conditions and prevent cheating, think about using different test versions. The test questions can be the same but in different orders. If you plan on giving the same test to multiple classes, change numbers or names. As much as you will tell students not to discuss test questions or answers, they will. Since students have easy access to various technology devices like cell phones and laptops, setting expectations of technology use is important. Some questions to consider:

- Should cell phones be collected and in a cell phone hotel?
- Should cell phones be away in backpacks?
- Will you allow students to wear headphones during a test?
- Where will students be seated during a test?
- Should students take off their smart watches?

Being proactive about student cheating helps to avoid it. If students do cheat, take their tests away at the moment but don't discipline students. You want to avoid confronting a student in front of others. You can also pull the student into the hallway or send them to the office. Being aware of the policies and procedures your school has in place will help you set up a plan.

Plagiarism is when a student uses someone else's work and claims it as their own. Similar to cheating, students will copy work and use it as their own when they lack the knowledge or time to complete an assignment. Now, with the introduction of AI, the lines of plagiarism are blurred. To avoid students plagiarizing, think about your assignments. Are the assignments easily "googleable"? Do the assignments require higher-order thinking? In the CTE field, having students complete a practical assessment where they must perform avoids plagiarism and requires students to actively demonstrate their skills. Recently, there were rubrics for AI use in the classroom that signals if students can use it in the project. Consider using a rubric or having a conversation with students about the use of AI. Be clear to your students about acceptable uses of AI. Communication is the first step in forming an understanding of expectations.

Grading and assessments is a complex and challenging topic. Effective grading transcends mere numbers and serves as powerful for communication, feedback, and student growth. Good grading and assessment practices contribute to student motivation and cultivates a growth mindset. Best practices better prepare students to be successful in the real world and have the tools to address potential challenges. At the core, you need to be open to change and embracing different ideas. Begin planning for a unit with the end of unit goals in mind. This simple practice will change your grading practices. It can be hard to shift a culture of grading and assessment in your school. Learn and explore different methods.

**Recommended Reading**

- *Grading Smarter, Not Harder* by Myron Dueck.
- *Making Grades Matter* by Matt Townsley and Nathan L. Wear.
- *How to Grade for Learning* by Ken O'Connor.

 **Discussion Questions**

- Beyond compliance, what is the core purpose of grades in your classroom? Do they primarily serve as a tool for communication, a motivator for learning, or a measure of mastery?
- How can a grading system be designed to truly assess "can they actually *do* it?" rather than just "do they know *about* it?"
- How do you ensure your assessments are valid (measuring what they are supposed to measure) and reliable (consistent)?
- How can you design your summative assessments to not only test knowledge, but also demonstrate a student's ability to apply skills in a practical, real-world context?
- What is one specific change you would consider making to your own grading practices after reflecting on the ideas in this chapter? What steps would you take to implement it?

| | |
|---|---|
| Student rolls eyes after teacher makes them work with someone. | Student constantly talks over teacher and other peers when they are presenting. |
| Student participates in class discussions by saying the following:<br>• Yes, I agree<br>• That was a good point<br>• Thanks for sharing | Student takes the initiative to share notes with students. |

| Student emails teacher about not understanding the assignment after it is due. | Student submits work on time but does not follow directions. |
|---|---|
| Student works on English, Math, or other homework while in CTE program. | Student occasionally hands in assignments late or forgets until reminded. |

Copyright material from Samantha Shane (2026), *The Secondary Educator's CTE Toolkit*, Routledge

|  |  |
|---|---|
| Student does not participate in class ever. | Student always completes homework and is prepared for class. |
| Student makes a joke while participating that isn't on topic or task. | Student is on cell phone when finished with work. |

| | |
|---|---|
| Student doesn't want to teach in the preschool five minutes before class starts. | Student is on laptop (but listening) when group work or someone is presenting. |
| Student is off task during group activity. | Student snickers when another student is talking |

| Student leaves materials in hallway or all over the classroom. | Student talks negatively about the Academy or teacher. |
| --- | --- |
| Student disrupts other classes when working on assignments outside the classroom. | Students talks negatively about a business partner or guest speaker |

Copyright material from Samantha Shane (2026), *The Secondary Educator's CTE Toolkit*, Routledge

# References

Advance CTE. (2023, November 23). *The Career Ready Practices*. Career Tech. https://careertech.org/document/the-career-ready-practices/

Brookhart, S. M. (2023). *Classroom Assessment Essentials*. ASCD.

Dueck, M. (2014). *Grading Smarter, Not Harder: Assessment Strategies that Motivate Kids and Help Them Learn*. ASCD.

Dueck, M. (2021). *Giving Students a Say: Smarter Assessment Practices to Empower and Engage*. ASCD.

Hattie, J. (2023). *Visible Learning: The Sequel: A Synthesis of Over 2,100 Meta-Analyses Relating to Achievement*. Routledge.

Link, L. J., & Guskey, T. R. (2022). Is standards-based grading effective? *Theory Into Practice*, 61(4), 406–417. https://doi.org/10.1080/00405841.2022.2107338

New Jersey Department of Education. (2025, May 13). *Career Readiness, Life Literacies & Key Skills*. New Jersey Student Learning Standards. www.nj.gov/education/standards/clicks/

O'Connor, K. (2017). *How to Grade for Learning: Linking Grades to Standards*. SAGE.

Rinkema, E., & Williams, S. (2018). *The Standards-Based Classroom: Make Learning the Goal*. SAGE.

Townsley, M., & Wear, N. L. (2020). *Making Grades Matter: Standards-based Grading in a Secondary PLC at Work*. Solution Tree.

Using Rubrics | Center for Teaching Innovation. (n.d.). *Center for Teaching Innovation*. Retrieved July 31, 2025. https://teaching.cornell.edu/teaching-resources/assessing-student-learning/using-rubrics

Wiliam, D., & Leahy, S. (2015). *Embedding Formative Assessment: Practical Techniques for K-12 Classrooms*. Learning Sciences International.

# 6

# Guest Speakers and Collaborating with Stakeholders

Guest speakers provide an opportunity for students to gain insight into different jobs, tasks in the field, and current job skills and information. Guest speakers can be the first look at a career for students and the first step toward gaining fundamental industry information. Guest speakers can be used to introduce a project, provide deeper learning during a project, or serve as a culminating experience for a unit. For example, having an Applied Behavior Analysis (ABA) therapist work with students in a career program focused on teaching, three times to learn about behaviors in the classroom. During the first visit, students learned the reason behind classroom behaviors and how to identify those behaviors. The ABA therapist had students observe preschoolers for two weeks before she returned. When she came back, she taught students how to analyze the data and make a behavior plan. After her second time coming in, students used the data they analyzed to create behavior plans and binders. On her final visit, she taught students how to use the behavior binders. The students gained numerous benefits from interacting with this guest speaker like a new possible career path, foundations of behavior management, and how to better support their future

DOI: 10.4324/9781003598053-7

students but what was the catalyst for partnering and planning with successful speakers?

The first step for identifying guest speakers is focusing on the goal of the class. When looking at the goal, consider what standard is the current focus in the class. Guest speakers can enhance and align with the CTE program standards and content, provide feedback on student work, and expose students to a career field. These relationships are foundational for students to make connections, expose themselves to the workforce, and experience careers. Start a spreadsheet with a list of the standards for each unit. I usually keep a list of possible guest speakers and contact information on a spreadsheet. Building a list of a myriad of guest speakers is important and allows for me to brainstorm different experiences. I keep another list of guest speakers that actually come each year, so at the end of the year or when my supervisor needs information for reporting to the state, it is readily available.

The power of relationships is a major theme of how to find guest speakers. I've had success by going to conferences, networking with others in the industry, and connections from parents. The best success I've had is by simply sending an email. By focusing on the standards first and seeing the purpose of the guest speaker, it will enhance the connection of the guest speaker and avoid confusion and lack of consistency with the students and their learning. It can also cause superficial content knowledge being learned. It can be overwhelming to brainstorm potential partners. In the first year of a program, start small with guest speakers. Intentionally plan one to two guest speakers for the year.

Looking closely at the language of the standards and the enduring understandings will provide strong direction to which guest speaker is beneficial for students and when to bring the guest speaker in. The following are standards from New Jersey's Law and Public Safety Career Pathway and possible guest speaker ideas.

Law and public safety career pathway (New Jersey Department of Education, 2025)

| Standard | Possible guest speakers | Collaboration ideas |
|---|---|---|
| Formulate ideas, proposals, and solutions to ensure effective and efficient delivery of law, public safety, corrections, and/or security services | - Detective or investigator to discuss problem-solving techniques<br>- Emergency management coordinator to explain how communities prepare and respond to disasters<br>- Correctional program manager to discuss the development and implementation of programs within a jail or prison setting | There are several ways to collaborate with guest speakers A guest speaker can task students with real scenarios they face to help solve a problem. For example, a fire marshall can task students with completing a community risk analysis to develop solutions to improve community safety |
| Analyze the role forensics plays in preventing and solving crimes | - Forensic scientists/ specialists<br>- Crime scene investigator<br>- Attorney | A guest speaker can help students through a mock crime scene investigation. In the scene, students can analyze evidence and learn techniques in forensics. Students are able to learn hands-on how to evaluate evidence and explain the role of forensics |

Thinking carefully about the purpose of the guest speaker creates purpose and deepens student learning. Guest speakers love to give back to students and help inspire the next generation of career professionals. Finding high-quality speakers that are also diverse and represent a variety of cultures, backgrounds, and people shows provides students with a range of perspectives, fosters empathy, deepens problem-solving, and challenges stereotypes. Guest speakers that have had different pathways to their profession showcase an opportunity for students to gain insight and understanding that different pathways can still mean success. Guest speakers are an exciting opportunity but ensuring they are timely and valuable is critical for the success of the partnership. Consider these questions when planning a guest speaker:

- What is the curriculum connection to what my students are learning?
- How can the guest speaker bring content to life and work with my students?
- What outcomes will the guest speaker provide for my students?

In the following table, you will find different CTE programs and example guest speakers.

| Business | Culinary | Cosmetology | Computer science | Education |
|---|---|---|---|---|
| Local business owners | Chefs from local restaurants | Local hairdressers | Software engineer | Teachers and guidance counselors |
| Social media marketers | Food suppliers | Makeup artists | Open source developer | Child therapists |
| Accountants | Authors of cookbooks | Estheticians | Cybersecurity expert | Child life specialists |
| CEOs of companies | Food scientists | Local salon owners | Tech startup | Teacher consultants |
| | Food sustainability advocate | Beauty suppliers | | Educational lawyer |

This list can expand and grow each year based on student interest and projects. Providing a range of guest speakers allows students to fully explore the career options. Survey students to see what kinds of guest speakers they would like to see throughout the year. Reach out to your local business and organization for different opportunities for guest speakers. Community members and parents are also willing to give back to the community. Surveying parents on back-to-school nights and posting on social media can harness powerful connections. Parent support and networking proves to be a beneficial factor when gaining guest speakers. Parents often have connections or are in the industry. Moreover, brainstorming a list with advisory council members can contribute to a well-rounded list of guest speaker ideas. This allows better planning and aligning the guest speaker to the goals of the CTE program. Money can be a factor when securing guest speakers. Some guest speakers will speak for free or charge a rate based on the speaking engagement. Different grants can provide opportunities for teachers to bring guest speakers into the classroom. Asking your administration if there are specific grants like Perkins available can be helpful when reaching out to guest speakers. Some schools have a specific guest speaker rate. Websites like Nepris and SpeakerHub offer a range of speakers at various costs, with the added benefit of free search options.

However, the power of networking shouldn't be underestimated. Other organizations like the Association for Career and Technical Education provide resources for CTE teachers to find guest speakers and connect to a large community. Networking can provide opportunities to share ideas and guest speakers. Lastly, doing research on local organizations and just reaching out via email can prove to be a strong method when looking for quality guest speakers. Typically, every profession has a local professional organization. When contacting guest speakers, provide context about the program and expectations. In the email, highlight the purpose of why they are speaking, specific dates, and contact information. Include key information about the students they will be working with and the amount of students. Having a call to be clear in expectations and the extent of the partnership is important. After the initial email, it is also important to ask about payment. If you have a budget, be honest about that number. Most guest speakers are willing to talk to students for free, and you can offer for them to post pictures on social media. Share the pictures with your district to post on social media as well. This provides an opportunity for the school to showcase its great partnerships and the guest speaker to gain recognition. If the guest speaker does require payment, ensuring you follow your school's procedure for submitting requests is essential for booking your guest speaker. Schools may require guest speakers to be board-approved as well. Reach out to your supervisor in writing to let them know about the guest speaker along with the goals and purpose.

Alumni of the program is a powerful way to gain guest speakers. Reach out to former students at various stages in their career to be guest speakers. Former students display a strong connection to the program and can offer valuable insights and advice to current students. It provokes students to think about their potential journeys and students enjoy the real-world connection. February is Career Technical Education Month. Consider planning guest speakers or an alumni panel to talk with students. It celebrates the importance of CTE and creates powerful connections for students. Prior to graduation, email your seniors a survey to complete. Questions should include evaluating the program and postgraduation plans. More importantly, ask students for their personal emails since school email accounts will be shut down. Try to send alumni emails at least each year to stay in touch. Have the students create a newsletter and send it.

Sample Email to Potential Guest Speaker:

*Dear Guest Speaker,*

*I hope you are doing well. I am an Education & Learning teacher at [insert school name]. My students are currently studying music education which includes how the brain develops and the benefits of music in the classroom. I am asking you to be a guest speaker in my classroom. Your expertise on music education and how the brain develops would greatly impact my students.*

*It would be ideal if you could demonstrate some strategies you use with our on-site preschool. We currently have 14 preschool students that my high school students work with weekly. We are available Mondays, Wednesdays, and Fridays between 9:20 and 10:45. Please let me know if you are interested and we can set up a time to talk more. I look forward to this partnership.*

*Best,*
*Samantha Shane*

After this initial email, the smaller details about a specific date, payment, and content are discussed. Sharing more specific information includes pertinent background information (if the students are Multilingual Learner, specific IEP needs, or if students have aides), current covered content students have learned, and technology students have available to them. When the planning of a guest speaker lacks vision and expectations, the results will negatively impact the program. Being specific and clear when identifying and contacting guest speakers is important. In the initial planning with a guest speaker, consider if the guest speaker is introducing new concepts, providing feedback on student learning, or helping to wrap up a unit. Suggesting ideas about the content students are currently learning allows for the guest speaker to better understand the vision for the collaboration. By understanding the current curriculum, the guest speaker can tailor their presentation to complement and reinforce the concepts students are already studying. This avoids redundancy and ensures that the guest speaker engagement adds value to the existing learning. It creates a cohesive learning experience where the guest speaker's expertise builds upon the foundation already laid in the classroom. Providing context allows the guest speaker to draw connections between the students' current learning and their own experiences and expertise. This helps students see the relevance of their studies to real-world careers and applications, making the learning more meaningful and motivating.

Guest speakers can also be recurring. When considering a guest speaker, think about the purpose and how the guest speaker can be incorporated to help enhance the curriculum. One example from a law-focused CTE program is having a lawyer review student's opening statements and questions for their mock trial. The lawyer initially came in and provided students with the overall process of a trial and then presented some tips for writing opening statements and how to cross examine. Two weeks later, the lawyer returned to provide feedback to students on their opening statements and questions for cross examination. When planning a recurring guest speaker, be sure to secure the multiple dates and plan each session with the guest speaker ahead of time. Consider the length of the project and be mindful of the guest speaker's time.

Further, sharing a guest speaker with colleagues and creating moments for interdisciplinary connections builds learning networking for students. Reach out to colleagues that might be in a similar unit, and their students can benefit from the same guest speaker. For example, health care and education listen to guest speakers from school social workers and the school psychologist together. When planning a potential interdisciplinary connection and guest speaker, be open with the guest speaker about the audience.

Lastly, survey students about their insight. A survey for ideas about who students might want to see can help you as the teacher gains student knowledge about their future goals and understanding of the material. This is also the place to start letting your students take the lead. Consider how to make this process more student- centered. How can your students take the lead on inviting guest speakers? How can students better interact with guest speakers? Providing students an opportunity to practice their career skills within their industry builds confidence but also fosters relationships that students need to grow. Networking is a key skill, and guest speakers are a good opportunity for students to practice this essential soft skill.

Always connect with the guest speaker to share the expectations, content, and structure of the session before the date agreed upon. The power of video calls has opened so many doors for speakers. With the different video call services, the access of guest speakers has increased. Video calling also eliminates the need for a speaker to travel, creating endless opportunities to connect throughout the world. When discussing the format with guest speakers, I often use Zoom or Google Meet because of my familiarity with and easy access to both platforms. Other platforms include Skype, Microsoft Teams, WhatsApp, and Slack.

Once you have a set date for the guest speaker, involve your students in preparing. I always send a calendar invite to the guest speaker and students in advance to ensure everyone is aware and committed to the date. Students will research the guest speaker prior to them coming, so our time is well spent. Students will brainstorm in small groups questions before sharing with the whole class. Each group will take a turn sharing a question they want to ask and one student will record the questions from all groups on a Google Doc. After students have created the list, they evaluate the questions and categorize them. In evaluating the questions, some questions are reworded, rewritten, or eliminated. By organizing the questions into categories, it helps students focus on what information they hope to gain from the guest speaker. Categories can be simple like education, advice, content, and daily work or more content specific. When creating questions, I tell the students to make a plan in creating questions. Here are some guidelines I give students:

- Avoid questions that have answers on Google.
- Make connections between their expertise and the content we are learning.
- Be specific in your question, avoid broad, general questions.
- Be respectful in how you ask your question.
- Questions should focus on the profession and industry, avoid personal questions.
- Show understanding of the topic by asking thoughtful questions.

Here is a list of sample questions:

- Can you describe a typical day at your job?
- What skills are most important for success in your field?

- What are the biggest challenges facing your industry right now?
- What advice do you have for students interested in this field?
- What is the role of [specific issue] in your industry?

Prior to the guest speaker arriving, I ask for a few volunteers to ask questions that are preplanned ahead of time. This helps limit the awkward silence that sometimes happens. As more guest speakers come in, students gain more confidence in asking questions. As a courtesy, I send the list of questions to the guest speaker ahead of time. Being clear about the timing, purpose, and questions helps the guest speaker have a meaningful session with the students. It maximizes time and creates a strong partnership for future collaborations. To ensure the guest speaker feels welcome upon arrival, I will assign roles like a greeter to meet the guest speaker in the front of the building and a notetaker. This student is charged with writing notes with the information shared, so we could revisit after the guest speaker. Preparing students for the guest speaker and setting expectations ensure a beneficial guest speaker experience. Tell your students what they should expect during the guest speaker. Setting high expectations for your students and explaining the purpose allow students to rise to the occasion, gain more from the experience, and grow their professionalism.

Documenting the experience is important. Be sure to take a few moments for photos with the guest speaker. Take pictures while the students are listening to the guest speaker or working with them. These pictures can be shared later on social media, newsletter, or with parents. You may have to gain special permission from parents ahead of time. Review your school's photo release policy before making promises to the guest speakers. One tip is to take photos from the back of the room where student faces are hidden. This highlights the guest speaker and shields student faces.

After the visit, students will reflect on what they learned. This can look like a project or writing assignment. I will also have students write a thank you which I send in a culminating email with any pictures I took. It is important to ensure your students have school media releases before sharing any pictures. Students also might revisit the notes for an extended assignment. For example, after the music teacher, students created a music lesson plan using the information and strategies they learned. In their lesson plan, they wrote a reflection on what strategies and brain development information they used. Sending a thank you email after the guest speaker has left is crucial for maintaining a relationship. Guest speakers can lead to new opportunities for students like internships in the future and potential jobs.

Unfortunately, there are times where guest speakers will cancel at the last minute or technology doesn't work. Having a backup plan is necessary to ensure students are still learning the material. Backup plans can include having a video of an interview with someone of a similar profession, a webquest about the industry, or exploring industry resources. As AI websites emerge, some offer functions that take on the role of a person or career. Students can sit in groups and chat with an AI tool that will take on the persona of the guest speaker.

Having a backup plan is important. Always having another space available or computer for technology issues also puts in place a plan. In education, we need to be flexible and prepared.

### Field Trips

Taking students on a field trip can truly enhance the learning experience for students. Taking students off campus to an industry location exposes students to a diverse range of industry occupations and understanding the workplace. A field trip validates what is learned in the classroom, leading students to deeper thinking. A CTE field trip should fit into one of the following categories:

- Direct connection to the curriculum
- CTSO or competition
- Workshop
- Exposure to the industry
  - Job shadowing
  - Tour of industry workplace

Planning field trips takes time and careful considerations. Similar to guest speakers, transparent communication with the location is important and time to ensure the field trip is approved. Talk about the expectations you have for students with the field trip location. Often, businesses are willing to design a custom experience for your students. If you are proposing a new experience, be specific. For example, a local museum hosts professional development for teachers. I contacted the department if my students can have a professional development workshop similar to the teachers. Most places are open to working together. Being familiar with the process and timeline to approval is the first step of planning. Typically, buses need to be secured, permission needs to be sent to parents, schools need to board approve the field trip, and payment needs to be secured.

As you plan your field trip, consider how many trips you will attend each year. If students need to miss class, you want to avoid making students miss their other classes. While the absence is sometimes excused, combined with student absences for being sick or other life events, it can add up how many classes they have missed. Your school should also have a testing calendar that has the dates for standardized testing. One way around missing multiple classes for students is planning trips during your class block. For example, my one class is 180 minutes long. My students and I are able to go to a local elementary school once a week, so students can push into classrooms. This eliminates students missing their other classes and still exposes them to industry experience. Be sure to review your school's safety procedures for a field trip and know student health information. Does a student require an inhaler, epipen, or medication at a certain time? What if a student needs to go to the hospital? Often, your school will have a student to chaperone ratio for field trips. If you are taking a chaperone, make sure they have all necessary information like your cell phone number, field trip agenda, and student information.

There are several tools to communicate with your students when on field trips without giving out your cell phone number. Remind serves as a way to "text" with students when on field trips. It is an application you can download on your phone but also control from a website on your laptop. Parents also have the option to join. Be sure to check with your school for recommendations on communicating with students. Whichever method you choose to use, be sure to clearly communicate with students how to get in touch with you.

I was working at a local museum to revise their curriculum for schools. The whole process was a lot of fun and the museum needed to pilot the program. I volunteered my students, seeing this as a great way for students to see another career within the field of education, provide feedback on curriculum and programming, and understand how to effectively present. I was so excited for my students to engage in this process, and I really made the field trip sound amazing. When we arrived at the museum, the staff greeted us and we started our evaluation of the program. Fifteen minutes into the program, I could feel my students' eyes in the back of my head. The presentation and execution of the program were not the best. It was clear the museum staff needed practice and tips for working with high school students. Unfortunately, not every field trip goes well or is well-received by the students. My students provided the staff with a ton of great feedback and solutions to some of the challenges the staff encountered. Ultimately, the staff of the museum revised their program and teaching practice. My students didn't let me forget about the field trip for 2 years. Sometimes, it is about admitting something wasn't the best and discussing what we learned from it. My students were able to take away how important it is to plan carefully and know your audience.

Another field trip my students have loved is visiting another CTE school. My students don't always get to interact with other students in a similar program. Once a year, I am able to collaborate with another CTE school that has a program. We take turns going to their school and then coming to us. At the school, we take a tour and have students design an agenda. This typically is a presentation on how each program runs and then students share ideas for ways to improve their program and different project ideas. It has sparked ideas on how to better collaborate, new curriculum projects, and ways to improve. It also provides my students with a community to talk about being a CTE student.

## Advisory Council

When creating a new CTE program or taking over one, the advisory council plays a critical role in guiding and enhancing the CTE program. While a requirement of receiving funding, advisory councils are composed of various stakeholders to establish the need of the program, make recommendations on budget and curriculum, and guide overall future of the program. It is also listed as a high-quality element from ACTE. It is recommended that partners ensure the program is meeting the current future workforce demand by reviewing the curriculum, identifying appropriate assessments and credentials, evaluating facilities, equipment, and materials, and providing work-based learning opportunities (High-Quality CTE Framework Development – ACTE Online, n.d.). People that sit on the advisory council include student, parent, school counselor, multiple industry connections, college or continuing education counselor, and work-based learning coordinator. Be sure to check with your school and state if they require a certain amount of industry connections. Networking is a powerful opportunity that students within CTE programs should be taking advantage of. The advisory council builds connections between the industry and students. By providing opportunities for students to interact with industry professionals, advisory councils can help students develop valuable relationships and gain insights into potential career paths. These connections can lead to internships, apprenticeships, job shadowing opportunities, and even job offers.

Finding professionals to serve on the advisory council can be overwhelming. Leveraging your current network and connections from the industry is the first step. If you are taking over a program that already has an advisory council, evaluate the current members. Invite them to continue sitting on the committee. Send the email, attend an event, or walk into a business. The Colorado Career and Technical Education recommends the following when contacting future members (Advisory Committee Development – Colorado Career and Technical Education, n.d.):

- ♦ Introduce yourself and role.
- ♦ State how you found the person.

- Talk about your program and what that person can bring to the advisory council.
- Give the time commitment and participation.
- Give contact information.

You may want to create a one-page document that highlights your program and the impact the advisory council has. The material could be used for open houses, talking to potential vendors, and while networking.

Next, asking current parents and students if they have any strong ties to the industry allows for meaningful connections and buy-in. Parents and students should also serve on the advisory council. When reaching out, be sure to be clear about the expectations of the advisory council. Another group to make use is the program alumni. If you are new to the school/CTE program, ask the school administration or counselors for the alumni contact information. Further, reaching out to local businesses and local professional associations and attending local industry events build connections. Many companies want a community connection and will be happy to sit on the advisory council. These companies often are eager to contribute to helping shape the future of the workforce. It also creates strong connections for students to apply for jobs if companies see how strong a CTE program is first hand. Lastly, making connections with post-secondary options to sit on the advisory council allows for robust relationships. These partners can offer a vital link in creating a rigorous program, so students can excel in their next steps.

Planning the biannual advisory council meetings should involve careful consideration for the needs and an intentional agenda. Since these meetings are often set at the beginning and end of the school year and time is limited, eliciting important discussions and recommendations requires a well-structured agenda. The CTE teacher is often responsible for the following:

- Identifying members for the advisory council.
- Planning and facilitating the meeting.
- Documenting the notes from the meeting.

♦ Informing members of program updates.
♦ Fostering communication with members throughout the year.

Prior to the meeting, creating a well-crafted agenda can help keep the meeting on track, ensure that all important topics are covered, and maximize the time available for discussion and decision-making is important. Sometimes, your supervisor might supply the agenda for all CTE programs if they are looking for specific feedback.

**Sample Agenda for a 1.5-hour Meeting**
6:00–6:10 – Introductions and Program Updates

Spend a few moments letting everyone introduce themselves. Members should share their role and business. During this time, update the council about any curriculum changes, enrollment updates, and major changes and take a tour of the classroom/shop.

6:10–6:30 – Topic 1

Pose each topic as a question to promote thought and discussion.

6:30–6:50 – Topic 2
6:50–7:20 – Topic 3
7:20–7:30 – Next Steps

Share any requests you have for members, upcoming projects, and future meeting dates.
Sample topics could include the following:

Current Workforce Trends
Curriculum Changes and Review
  Budget Review and Funding Challenges
  Equipment and Facility Updates

Technology Guidance
Community Partnerships
Career-Ready Practices
Guest Speakers and Demonstrations
Celebrate Student Success Stories
Work-Based Learning
Mentorship Programs
Industry Certifications

At the beginning of the first yearly meeting, take time to give the council a tour. This tour can highlight new tools, curriculum, or space. It allows the members to fully understand the program before discussing the topics for the night. The tour also demonstrates how important the program is. Many industry professionals and parents become impressed and buy-in during this moment. If alumni are present, they can share a success story that was a result of attending the program. Capturing the discussion and ideas from the meeting is important. Have a student write notes using a laptop to review and memorialize the discussion. School administrators may ask for a copy of these notes for reporting purposes, particularly to secure federal funding (such as through the Perkins V grant) and for program verification during audits. These documents serve as tangible proof that your program is actively engaged with the local business community and is continuously aligning its curriculum with industry needs. Be sure to review your school and state's specific protocols, as they often require particular sections for documentation, such as a list of attendees, motions made and seconded, and a record of action items. Additionally, it's vital to recognize that program evolution is inevitable. Significant program changes might happen when you are part of the program, and the advisory council is your most valuable asset in navigating this process. This might look like a planned expansion to meet a growing demand, such as adding more sections or a new pathway. Conversely, it could be a complete curriculum revamp due to unforeseen circumstances, like a local industry shifting its technology or a new regulation changing safety requirements. By consistently and meticulously documenting the council's feedback and recommendations, you build a powerful case for these changes, demonstrating that they are not just your ideas, but are data-driven and supported by industry professionals. Well-documented advisory council meetings are the backbone of a high-quality CTE program. They provide the evidence needed to secure funding, justify resource requests, and, most importantly, ensure that your program remains dynamic and responsive to the needs of both students and the local economy.

While CTE advisory councils are designed to be a vital link, sometimes there are obstacles that can limit the effectiveness. Sometimes, there is difficulty attracting members from a broad range of industries. Further, some industry professionals might be excited to join but the distance and/or meeting time could negatively impact. If distance and time are problem, send the date out for the meeting as soon as you can. This ensures people can make arrangements in advance. Another option is hosting one meeting on Zoom or another video conferencing software. This allows members from all over to participate. Lastly, consider what time you are hosting the meeting. Some industries lend themselves better to day time meetings, whereas other industries prefer a later meeting. Other common problems could be dominating voices, focusing on the past vs. future, and showing reluctance to change.

To encourage a diverse advisory council, consider reaching out to different voices that might be interested. Tap into businesses that have hosted interns in the past and contact local chapters of industry-specific organizations. When communicating with the advisory council members, you can suggest ways they can interact with the program beyond meetings. Send out the meeting agenda beforehand.

If dominating voices happens to be an issue, continue to bring the discussion back to actionable outcomes. This focus allows participants to have a shared goal and limits the focusing on past practice. As the facilitator, you can implement a protocol to hear all voices. This could include a formal protocol, time limits, or speaking limits. Set the expectations and meeting norms at the start of the meeting. Like in our classrooms, our attitudes give off energy. As the CTE teacher, we need to cultivate a culture of openness and a future focused mindset. The rest of the advisory council will follow the lead.

### Student Advisory Council

While the main advisory council usually has only one to two students, creating a student-run advisory council creates leadership opportunities for the students. It also creates strong buy-in for students and fosters a culture of collaborations and belonging. Student advisory councils will bring issues to the table, plan fundraisers, recommend projects, and plan program events. Each year, students can complete an application process to be a member of the advisory council. Allowing students from various grade levels to be part of this council creates strong connections and smoother transitions.

Set a schedule to meet with students once a month. Use the school calendar to plan meetings for the entire school year. Providing the dates in advance demonstrates the importance of the meetings and sends clear communication to all participants. Encourage students to lead the meeting after setting the expectations and norms of the council. Further, having order to the meeting and a sense of purpose is critical to avoid complaining or negative undertones. Each meeting should have a clear purpose and structure. Fostering a sense of belonging and leadership creates opportunities for students to show up and be part of something. It enables students to gain a better understanding of themselves, cultivate self-confidence, and deepen their collaboration skills. Moreover, it provides a platform for students to voice their opinion, demonstrates their curiosity and dedication, and builds a stronger community.

### Possible Topics for Meetings

- ◆ Program Curriculum and Skills Development
  - ◆ Suggestions for new skills and areas to expand on.
  - ◆ Reviewing current curriculum: what's working and what could be improved.
  - ◆ Ideas for projects.

- Professional Learning and Guest Speakers
  - Identify specific industry professionals or alumni for talks/workshops.
  - Discuss desired certifications or credentials,
  - Brainstorm topics for future professional learning opportunities and field trips.
- Fundraisers and Grants
  - Design and create fundraisers to increase funding.
  - Create a wish list of items to purchase.
- Mentorship and Peer Initiatives
  - Creating peer activities for different grade levels.
  - Brainstorm ways to support students within the program.
  - Create a peer mentoring system.
- Safety Review
  - Review shop/classroom safety rules and suggest improvements.
- Program Outreach
  - Identify strategies to recruit new students to the program.
  - Develop promotional materials.
  - Plan presentations.

These topics can be modified based on the needs, trends, and student ideas. The goal of the student advisory council is to build capacity, whereas the advisory council is to build the future of the program and keep current with industry trends. The student advisory council members are usually different from the one to two students on the advisory council. It provides multiple leadership opportunities and a chance for students to develop their skills.

## Application Questions

The application helps give you insight on student thinking and who is serious about being on the advisory council. When deciding to roll out the Student Advisory, be sure to explain the expectations before students apply. Be open and honest about the application process, how members are selected, the time commitment, and student expectations. There are many different questions to ask and ways to collect responses. You can have students interview with a panel of educators, complete a video application, or answer questions on a Google Form. When designing the application, consider what information you really want to receive from students. You can also include skills you find important to your industry and have students rate their skills and explain why. I like asking students to rate their skills to practice self-reflection and highlight their areas of growth. The following are a few sample questions to include on the application:

- Why do you want to be part of the student advisory council?
- What are your top three strengths and why?
- Write about a time you had conflict with someone else and how you resolved it.
- What other school commitments do you have (sports, clubs, work, etc.).
- Program specific questions/scenarios: The following are two broad examples of scenario-based questions.
    - If you could implement one new project or activity in our program, what would it be and why? How would it benefit other students?
    - You are working on a team project, and one team member is consistently not contributing their part. How do you address this situation to ensure the project's success and maintain positive dynamics?
    - Why do you believe that the student voice is important in shaping our CTE program? How would you ensure the council represents the diverse opinions of all students?
    - Students are talking negatively about the program and seem frustrated with the teacher. How would you handle these students talking?
    - Students in your class are really eager to learn more about a specific skill, but it isn't in the syllabus provided by the teacher. What could you do?

You can develop a rubric to help score the applications, ask a trusted colleague to help choose, or include your advisory council in choosing students. Reviewing applications and selecting students can be difficult if there is an overwhelming response.

Overall, providing students with a variety of authentic experiences is essential for bridging the critical gap between classroom instruction and real-world application. From inviting guest speakers to share their expertise and career paths, to organizing hands-on field trips that bring concepts to life and facilitating structured work-based learning experiences, these opportunities immerse students in the industry. Such engagements are vital for students to gain firsthand insights, practice professionalism, and develop the highly sought-after skills that employers consistently demand. By creating multiple pathways for students to interact with professionals and the industry, CTE teachers are not just teaching a subject; they are effectively building a direct pipeline to future success, ensuring students are not only prepared for a career but are also confident and connected from day 1.

## Recommended Reading

- *School, Family, and Community Partnerships: Your Handbook for Action* by Joyce L. Epstein.
- *Building School-Community Partnerships: Collaboration for Student Success* by Mavis G. Sanders.
- *The Joyful Teacher* by Berit Gordon.

## Discussion Questions

- What is the purpose of guest speakers in my classroom? What specific learning objectives or skills do you hope to reinforce by inviting a guest speaker?

- How can you transition a single guest speaker visit into a long-term partnership? What are some potential models for project-based collaboration, mentorship, or ongoing professional consultation that could extend beyond the classroom?
- What advisory council members are critical to enhancing our program?
- How do you ensure your advisory council's composition is diverse and truly representative of the local industry, including small businesses and emerging fields?

## References

Advisory Committee Development – Colorado Career and Technical Education. (n.d.). Colorado CTE. Retrieved July 31, 2025. https://coloradostateplan.com/administrator/advisory-committee/advisory-committee-development/

High-Quality CTE Framework Development – ACTE Online. (n.d.). Association for Career and Technical Education. Retrieved July 31, 2025. www.acteonline.org/professional-development/high-quality-cte-tools/high-quality-cte-development/

New Jersey Department of Education. (2025, May 13). *Career Readiness, Life Literacies & Key Skills*. New Jersey Student Learning Standards. www.nj.gov/education/standards/clicks/

# 7

# Working with Diverse Learners

**Terms to Know:**

**Individual Education Plan (IEP)** – legally binding document created for each public school child who is eligible for special education services under the Individuals with Disabilities Education Act (IDEA). It is a written statement that outlines the child's unique educational needs, goals, and the specific services and supports the school will provide to help the child learn.

**504 Plan** – Focuses primarily on providing the necessary supports for the student to access the general education curriculum and participate in school activities.

As a teacher, we have an innate passion for wanting to help others. This can include providing students with snacks because they don't have access to food at home, giving students school supplies because their families struggle, giving students extra help after school or at lunch time, or simply just providing a space for students to be themselves. Teachers care deeply about their students and try to move mountains for them to become successful. Each student comes to our classroom with a different strength and challenge. The one-size-fits-all approach doesn't work anymore. Today's students are different in a good way; they are able to identify their own strengths, have access to endless resources, and continue to navigate challenges in our world. This chapter dives deeper into students who require tailored support, yet bring immense potential to the classroom. We will explore how to effectively meet the diverse needs of students with special education classifications, students with 504 plans, those diagnosed with ADHD, English language learners, and students who have experienced Adverse Childhood Experiences (ACE). By understanding their unique strengths and challenges and implementing targeted strategies, educators can ensure every student has the opportunity to thrive and reach their full potential.

Understanding the process of providing support to students and how to best support students with IEPs, 504 plans, or English language learners can help foster a successful outcome for the student. According to the Office for Civil Rights, in 2020–2021, there were a total of 8.4 million students with disabilities enrolled in the United State's public schools. This accounts for 17% of the overall student enrollment (CRDC Profile of Students with Disabilities in U.S. Public Schools During the 2020-21 School Year, n.d.). Further, research shows that Career and Technical Education (CTE) programs better support and set students with disabilities up for success than traditional programs. Students with disabilities in a CTE course are more likely to graduate and be employed within 2 years of graduation (Theobald et al., 2022, p. 40). This success is often attributed to CTE's inherent hands-on, applied learning environment, its direct relevance to career goals, and the emphasis on practical, tangible skills which often resonate well with different learning styles.

Trying to navigate how to support students that have been identified with an IEP, 504 plan, and more may be overwhelming. Ensuring that all students are getting their needs met by the teacher is not only important, but it is a legal obligation for educators. A thorough understanding of best practices is essential for teachers to meet their legal responsibility of upholding IEPs and providing optimal student support. This chapter aims to provide educators with a basic overview of supporting students in the classroom. However, the best support and learning come from working with your district's special education department.

## History of IEP and IDEA

The IDEA, Section 504 of the Rehabilitation Act of 1973 (Section 504), and the American with Disabilities Act (ADA) each provide federal legislation to support the education of individuals with disabilities (Congress Research Service). Schools under IDEA need to ensure students receive a free appropriate public education (FAPE). The IDEA is the main governing body that oversees special education for children from birth through age 21 and imposes requirements on public schools. In 2023, 7.6 million children ages 3 through 21 received special education services (Dragoo, 2024).

IDEA clearly defines what a disability is. First, it identifies a child having at least one condition in the 13 categories. The requirement is that it must "adversely affect a child's educational performance". Disabilities that do not impact a student's education do not qualify (Dragoo, 2024). To determine if a child is eligible in one of the 13 categories, the child needs to go through an evaluation process by a qualified staff member. The evaluation includes an individual psychological evaluation, social history, observations of students in educational settings, educational evaluation, and sometimes a physical examination (DeLussey, 2024, p. 10). The disability must adversely affect educational performance, and the child needs special education services to make progress in school (DeLussey, 2024, p. 11). Since IDEA legally protects children with defined disabilities, there are specific policies and procedures to identify and evaluate children who have a qualifying disability. After a child is found eligible, a team of professionals at the school meet to create an IEP for the student. The 13 categories are as follows:

- Specific learning disability
- Speech or language impairment
- Other health impairment
- Autism
- Intellectual disability
- Emotional disturbance
- Developmental delay
- Multiple disabilities

- Hearing impairment
- Orthopedic impairment
- Visual impairment
- Traumatic brain injury
- Deaf-blindness

According to the National Center for Learning Disabilities, dyslexia, dysgraphia, and dyscalculia are all specific learning disabilities that affect an individual's capacity to excel and are the most common (Specific Learning Disabilities, n.d.). They typically affect students' reading, writing, and math skills. Dyslexia primarily impacts reading; people struggle to recognize and blend sounds, as well as read and spell accurately. In the CTE classroom, this might manifest as challenges reading safety manuals, understanding written directions, following recipes. When students have dysgraphia, they have trouble producing writing that has structure and clarity. This could impact their ability to document project steps, label diagrams, take notes, or complete logbooks. Lastly, dyscalculia impacts a students' math skills (Specific Learning Disabilities, n.d.). In the CTE classroom, students may struggle to interpret data, understand ratios, calculate materials costs, or provide precise measurements. While these learning disabilities present challenges, it highlights the power of CTE's hands-on, visual, and applied learning environment.

Additionally, students with disabilities are entitled to be educated in the least restrictive environment (LRE) under the Individuals with IDEA. The principle of LRE guarantees a student's right to be educated in a setting that provides maximum opportunity to interact with their same-age, non-disabled peers and engage with the general education curriculum (DeLussey, 2024, p. 101). This placement is not a one-size-fits-all solution; it is determined by the IEP team based on the student's unique needs. The law requires a continuum of placements be available, beginning with the least restrictive and moving to the most (DeLussey, 2024, p. 102). The team must first consider the general education classroom with supplementary aids and services. If that environment is not appropriate, a student might receive push-in support, move to a co-teaching model, and then move to a resource room for part of the day. The continuum progresses to more restrictive settings like self-contained classrooms, specialized schools, and, finally, residential programs, which are only considered when a student's needs cannot be met in any less restrictive setting (DeLussey, 2024, p. 103).

Teachers play a critical role in the IEP process by providing feedback on students. Further, teachers need to maintain confidentiality of the IEP and 504 plans. It should only be discussed with those who are directly involved with that student. It is inappropriate to discuss it with another teacher that doesn't have that student. Within the IEP are different sections that help portray an understanding of the student. Since the IEP is a legally binding document, there are several sections to ensure the needs of the child are being met. Some sections include the following:

- Current Performance: This is also known as the present levels of educational performance. The information included is evaluation results from classroom tests, individual tests given during eligibility, and observations made by parents and teachers.
- Annual Goals: Each year, there are short-term objectives that are set that the student can reach within the year. Goals might address different academic, behavior, physical, or social emotional needs. The goals are measurable.
- Special Education and Related Services: In this section, you will find all services the student will receive. It will also include the modifications the student will need for the program.
- Transition Services: This section discusses the next steps for the student after high school graduation. The CTE teacher might be involved with educating everyone on the different options (Archived: IEP Guide Relating to IDEA 97 (Does Not Apply to Newer IDEA 2004 Reauthorization) (PDF), n.d.).

While the IEP might seem overwhelming, it is important to understand how to best serve the student. Understanding how to read the IEP and use the proper terminology is important. In each IEP and 504 plan are listed accommodations and modifications.

These are supports put in place during the IEP meeting that are recommended by educators, doctors, and parents. The supports aim to help students be successful in their classes. Each teacher that has the student is responsible for reviewing the IEP/504 plans and ensuring all supports are implemented. Each student has a case manager that oversees the student. Typically at the beginning of each school year, the case manager will hold time for teachers to review the IEP and ask questions before signing off on the IEP. This is different from the annual IEP meeting held each year and required by law.

The terms accommodations and modifications are often used synonymously but have major differences. Accommodations assist the student in learning. They aim to remove barriers and increase students learning the content (Twachtman-Cullen & Twachtman-Bassett, 2011, pp. 80–82). Accommodations are usually made to introduce methods, classroom assignments, time requirements, student output, or environment (Twachtman-Cullen & Twachtman-Bassett, 2011, p. 81). Accommodations do not change the curriculum materials. Modifications make changes to what the student learns (Twachtman-Cullen & Twachtman-Bassett, 2011, p. 82). Learning standards are modified so students can meet them. Understanding each accommodation and modification is important. You are legally mandated to provide the accommodations and modifications to students. The following are some accommodations and modifications. This does not reflect the full scope of accommodations and modifications that can be on a student's plan.

| Accommodations | Modifications |
| --- | --- |
| ♦ Providing audio/recordings of texts<br>♦ Testing in small group setting<br>♦ Preferential seating<br>♦ Extended time on test<br>♦ Giving copy of class notes<br>♦ Use of calculator<br>♦ Take sections of a test instead of all at once | ♦ Assigning fewer problems for students to solve<br>♦ Rewarding materials<br>♦ Assigning a different project |

What to expect during an IEP annual review meeting?

The IEP is reviewed once a year and requires an IEP meeting by federal law.

Prior to the meeting, the case manager for the student with the IEP will ask for feedback on the student. This will often involve detailed observations on what accommodations and modifications the student is currently using, which ones are proving ineffective or are not being utilized, and any recommended adjustments to better support their learning. Typically, the feedback includes a few focus areas which are: academic progress, observations and data, and any changes in performance. Provide specific examples of the student's strengths and weaknesses in the classroom. Be objective and specific as IEPs are legal documents. Feedback is put on the IEP. In offering examples, refer to assessment scores, work samples, or observation notes. Analyze any trends or patterns that have emerged. If students are not using specific accommodations and modifications, explain why. When writing feedback, these are some questions/things to consider the following:

- What are the student strengths?
- What are some challenges for the students?
- Organizational skills of the student.
  - Does the student come prepared to class?
  - Can the student organize their work space?
- Functional skills of the student.

Throughout the school year, documentation of advocating for students is important for ensuring the student's needs are being met and demonstrate a need for the help. After parent phone calls, send a follow-up email summarizing the call and citing next steps creates accountability, prevents confusion, and provides a written record of the conversation in the future. By creating a "paper trail" of all the communications can demonstrate how the school has worked with the parent and student to provide accommodations and modifications. Additionally, documenting providing accommodations and modifications can serve as proof of helping a child. For example, some students may require a copy of class notes, study guide, or articles ahead of time. Emailing the student with a digital copy of the notes, study guide, or article helps ensure students are receiving the accommodation but also protects the teacher from scrutiny.

There are several important members on the IEP team that include the following: child's parent, one general education teacher, one special education teacher, school counselor, and usually a member from the child study team. Students are also invited to be part of their own IEP meeting. Students participate in all or part of the meeting, as deemed applicable by team members (Intention IEP, p. 15). Some parents choose to bring an education advocate or lawyer to the meeting if they feel the school is not meeting the needs of their child. At the start of the IEP meeting, all members present will introduce themselves and the case manager will begin. During the IEP meeting, parents typically provide feedback on the student outside of school and struggles they see at home. Feedback will be provided by the case manager and other teachers in attendance. It is important to bring work samples, test results, or anecdotal evidence to present to the parents. The team will review the accommodations and make new recommendations if necessary.

The IEP meeting is a good benchmark to review the students' progress. However, waiting until the IEP meeting to update parents or raise concerns should be avoided. Communicating concerns early in the student's learning creates a strong relationship and better helps the student. During the IEP meeting, be open about the student's performance. Being prepared with specific examples helps explain and provides evidence of the student's current level. Try to avoid industry jargon and be inclusive. Discuss what accommodations and modifications work well for the student.

**Transition Planning**
IDEA states that transition services for students must be addressed no later than the first IEP when the child turns 16. Transition services then must be updated each year. The purpose is to help students with IEPs prepare for life after graduation.

Goals are typically in four different areas, vocational training, post-secondary education, jobs and employment, and independent living (Lee, n.d.). As a CTE teacher, your expertise is key to helping the student. By setting measurable goals in these areas, the transition plan ensures that students are not just graduating, but are actively preparing for their chosen path.

## Working with an Inclusion Teacher

Since children with IEPs are required to be in the LRE, they are placed in an inclusion classroom. Inclusion classrooms consist of students with IEPs and students without IEPs. In an inclusion classroom, there are two teachers to help support all students. One teacher is typically the subject area expert, and the other teacher is a certified special education teacher. One misconception is that inclusion teachers will only work with the special education students. This is not true, and in the stronger inclusion classes, students cannot tell which teacher is in the inclusion teacher and which is the general education. Inclusion classrooms provide a rich learning environment where students benefit from diverse perspectives and a collaborative learning experience. Students are able to gain valuable social and emotional skills.

To create a strong relationship with the inclusion teacher, start with open communication. Setting a time to meet with the inclusion teacher to explain your classroom expectations, classroom procedures, and upcoming assignments leads to a stronger partnership. Ask them for feedback and ideas on the upcoming assignments. While they may not have the content knowledge, having a different perspective could enhance the project for all students. Ideally, co-creating the classroom procedures and expectations is better in creating a strong classroom culture and relationship.

Some schools may have special education teachers push into the CTE classroom, serving as invaluable allies and partners in helping students with disabilities succeed. While this direct inclusion may not always be feasible in every CTE classroom, there are several proactive ways to better foster a robust collaborative relationship with the special education department and teachers in your school. By actively engaging with them, CTE teachers can ensure more effective support for all learners:

- Proactively share your curriculum/upcoming units.
    - Ask for advice on modifying a test, project, or classroom assignment.
    - This allows the special education teacher to anticipate any concerns and suggest strategies or resources. Be specific when you ask a question and pinpoint your challenge. For example, "I'm worried about Student A handling the multistep directions the practical".
- Review IEP together and ask questions about the accommodations.
    - Discuss the purpose behind some accommodations. I've received emails saying "Student B's work should be on a 20% work reduction". What exactly does that mean? Do I pick and choose which assignments Student B doesn't complete? Being clear about why and how can help you better work with the student.
    - Share feedback to the case manager about what accommodations seem to be working or not working in your classroom. This allows for positive problem-solving and clear communication. It also helps in best supporting the student.
- Seek strategies for specific learning challenges.
    - Inquire about specific learning disabilities and common challenges. It helps you learn different supports beyond the general accommodations.
- Invite special education teachers or case manager to observe you.
    - It can be scary to ask another professional adult to observe you. However, if you seem to be struggling, want advice on how to better help students, or need relevant advice, invite a special education teacher to observe you. The observation could be a specific part of your classroom routine or when you work one on one with students. It also allows the special education teacher to give more timely and relevant advice.

By protectively reaching out and building these relationships, you can transform potential challenges into opportunities, ensuring all students regardless of their learning difference have equitable access to high-quality CTE experiences.

## Section 504

Section 504 is similar to IDEA in that it helps to provide equal access to programs. Section 504 seeks to provide meaningful access to educational programs but does not provide funding for people with disabilities like IDEA does (Dragoo, 2024). Under Section 504, the definition for an individual with a disability is any person who has a physical or mental impairment that substantially limits one or more major life activities (Dragoo, 2024). 504 plans provide accommodations to students with disabilities such as migraines, anxiety, asthma, diabetes, and physical impairments like a broken leg to name a few. These plans are covered under the civil rights law, Section 504 of the Rehabilitation Act (Vierstra & Garcia, 2024). While 504 plans are legal documents, each school has their own format and process for 504 plans. You can typically find your school's 504 process on your school's website and handbook. 504 plans can also be temporary, for example, when a student has a broken bone or lasts several years.

Students with a 504 plan primarily focus on accommodations. They are changes to how a student learns or is assessed. Some common accommodations are similar to ones in an IEP, for example, extended time on tests, preferential seating, verbal prompts, and opportunity to see the nurse as needed. While 504 plans are less formal and detailed than IEPst, they don't include annual goals, present levels of performance, or transition services. Teachers are still legally required to comply with and follow all outlined accommodations for the student. If your student has a 504 plan, you should expect to still give feedback on the effectiveness of the accommodations and how the student is performing. Share observations about whether the accommodations are truly helping the students access the curriculum and demonstrate their learning. Take the time to really understand each student's 504 plan carefully. Familiarize yourself with the accommodations and how they apply in your classroom. Don't hesitate to reach out to the 504 case manager, school counselor, or your supervisor for help. Always maintain confidentiality of a student's 504 plan. Only share information with a staff member who has a need to know regarding the student.

**Working with an Aide**

Some students require a one-on-one aide that is referred to as a paraprofessional. They provide crucial support to help the individual student. The aide could be responsible for a variety of supports like implementing behavior plans, redirecting the students, assisting with mobility issues, helping students understand social cues, and much more. If you have an aide in your classroom, be sure to set time to discuss the student they work with. Aides are typically experts on that students' specific needs, triggers, and learning styles. The conversation you have should be centered around shared goals for the student.

Communication is key to effective collaboration. Establish a regular check-in routine with the aide, so you can share observations, successes, and challenges. This feedback is invaluable for adapting your teaching strategies. It will also be helpful to discuss the clearly defined roles. Consider who will be contacting parents if there is an issue in class or who is handling discipline. Discussing how the aide can best support your classroom management and instructional goals will ensure everyone is on the same page and prevent misunderstandings. Ask for their input on effective strategies when working with the student. Lastly, be sure to treat them with respect as they are a professional colleague. Their contribution is fundamental to the student's success. Behavior management in a CTE setting often involves redirecting students safely and efficiently amid tools and ongoing projects. The paraprofessional can be instrumental in proactive redirection and de-escalation, helping maintain focus while ensuring safety. In a hands-on environment, the paraprofessional is uniquely positioned to collect observational data on a student's progress toward IEP or 504 goals related to motor skills, task completion, following instructions, or social interactions within a team project.

**How do you meet the needs of accommodations when other students may think it is unfair?**
There will be some accommodations that students receive that may seem unfair to other students. It is important to never tell other students about another student's 504 plan, IEP, or any personal information. Some accommodations can help all students like providing a copy of notes for all students, breaking down assignments into meaningful tasks, repeating directions, and positive reinforcements. There is no rule stating you can't provide these supports for all students. More importantly, from the start of school, establish a classroom that acknowledges that each student has different learning preferences.

**How do you discipline students with diverse needs?**
School rules and policies apply to all students in the school. Students with IEPs and 504 plans have extra protections under IDEA. When a student with an IEP misbehaves, talk to your supervisor about how to handle the issue. The IEP or 504 team will write a Manifestation Determination to determine if the behavior was caused by the child's disability and was the behavior caused by the school's failure to implement the IEP or 504 plan (DeLussey, 2024, p. 31). During this time, the team will review the incident and look at the evidence. The team carefully reviews the incident, the student's file, and the implementation of their plan. The outcome of this review dictates whether the student can be disciplined like their peers or if the team must instead focus on providing the necessary behavioral interventions to support the student's success (DeLussey, 2024, p. 31).

## Students with ADHD
ADHD is a common condition that makes it hard for someone to focus, become easily distracted, and sometimes manage emotions (ADHD, 2023). There are many misconceptions about students with ADHD. The National Institutes of Health, the Centers for Disease Control and Prevention, and the American Psychiatric Association all recognize ADHD. While people with ADHD have trouble focusing and become easily distracted, when a person with ADHD is really interested in something, they can

have intense focus. Beyond focus and distractibility, ADHD also impacts executive functions, which are the brain's management skills. This can manifest as challenges with planning, organizing materials, managing time, prioritizing tasks, and regulating impulses or emotions. Understanding these broader impacts helps educators provide more comprehensive support. There are some common accommodations for students with ADHD like, using flexible seating, designating a quiet work space in the classroom, posting a written schedule, providing an extra set of books to keep at home, giving directions out loud and in writing, providing a lesson outline, and breaking assignments up into chunks (Morin & Osewalt, 2024).

From my own experience, the CTE classroom allows students with ADHD to thrive. They are able to move around, work with their hands, and dive into a project. However, students with ADHD can also be distracted in a CTE shop by ambient noise, visual clutter, the movement of other students, or multiple ongoing projects. Understanding your students' individual triggers is critical.

Some strategies to help with students are as follows:

- Structured Access to Tools/Materials: Being extremely organized is important in the classroom. Teaching students how to organize their materials is helpful in teaching them key skills. Limit access to tools students need for their current project. This allows them to focus on the current project.
- Defined Workstations: Similar to a desk, designating a specific workplace for each student or group creates a zone of focus.
- Visual Checklists and Timers: Using a checklist allows students to start taking accountability for themselves while keeping them on task. Timers displayed in the classroom or at the workstation allow students to manage their time.
- Use Competition: Students typically are drawn to competing. Introducing challenges or competitions often lead to focused students.
- Offered Structured Breaks: Beyond just breaking, students can benefit from a quick walk, using a stress

ball, or a mindfulness video. This can help students regulate before returning to a task.

It is absolutely inappropriate and a violation of privacy to ask students if they have taken their medication or to suggest they go on medication. These are personal medical decisions to be discussed solely between the student, their family, and healthcare professionals. Your role as an educator is to provide an inclusive learning environment and appropriate accommodations, regardless of a student's medical choices. Similarly, it is never okay to blame a student for something based on their ADHD. Their behaviors are often a result of their neurological differences, not a lack of effort or defiance. Instead, focus on problem-solving strategies and fostering a supportive environment that helps them manage their challenges.

## English Learners/Multiple Lingual Students

In 2021, 5.3 million students were learning English as a language (COE – English Learners in Public Schools, n.d.). These students are often referred to as English language learners or multilingual learners (MLs). Learning another language while completing high school graduation requirements can be challenging. Studies repeatedly show that proficiency in another language depends on how early in life someone began speaking it (Sousa, p. 169). While these students should receive pull out support, understanding how to best help these students while in your classroom and support their language development is key. More importantly, research shows that when MLs participate in CTE, it leads to great rates of high school completion, obtainment of postsecondary education, and earning higher wages. MLs also have higher growth potential in fields like technology, engineering, and health care (Career and Technical Education: Preparing K–12 Multilingual Learners for Postsecondary Education and Careers, n.d.).

Upper Bucks County Technical School (UBCTS) created an initiative to leverage student's knowledge of a language to enhance their job prospects. This program, Language as an Asset, prepares students for the multilingual demands of today's job markets by credentialing student language ability, using the American Council on the Teaching of Foreign Languages (ACTFL) and Assessment of Performance toward Proficiency in Languages (AAPPL). This proficiency test is beyond a basic vocab test but assesses the applied use of language in real-life settings. Their focus remains around several key objectives. First, UBCTS establishes that language proficiency is vital for career success. Second, they use comprehensive language tools to implement assessments to measure students' language abilities, and they integrate language training into the CTE curricula. Third, students are able to earn credentials like the Seal of Biliteracy and the official ACTFL certificates, a legally defensible credential recognized in public, private, and government sectors. When students exit UBCTS CTE programs, they can be dual certified, in their CTE skill area and in a language, setting them apart from other graduates entering the workforce.

Executive Director of UBCTS and ACTE Region 1 Vice-President Elect, Michael Herrera is dedicated to expanding CTE access to students and aims to remove barriers so students can gain real-world experience. He knows there are several industries that need multilingual employees. For example, in healthcare settings, language barriers can lead to delayed treatment, medical errors, or misdiagnosis. Imagine a student who, thanks to this program, can confidently assist a Spanish-speaking patient during a medical internship. Language proficiency builds cultural competency, critical thinking, and empathy, making students not just technically skilled, but globally aware and adaptable professionals.

Michael understands there are many challenges to overcome when schools are working with multilingual students. Some of these challenges include scheduling conflicts, families not being aware of programs, CTE teachers having a lack of support, transportation issues, and students needing certain prerequisites for CTE. He recommends starting by identifying students with language skills through school admissions paperwork and through surveys. Partner with employers to align language proficiency with workforce needs. Lastly, schools need to provide professional development for teachers, so they can support multilingual students in their programs. UBCTS's model could be a blueprint for other CTE centers looking to address similar workforce needs and support multilingual students. Michael's passion for removing barriers and expanding CTE access is the driving force behind this innovative approach, as he firmly believes that language should be a bridge, not a barrier, to opportunity.

There is also financial support to hire staff to help provide support to multilingual students. Within the Strengthening Career and Technical Education for the 21st Century Act (Perkins V), English learners are identified as a special population. This includes recruiting and supporting English learners to CTE programs (Perkins Briefs: English Learners, n.d.).

There are many strategies to help support ML CTE students to ensure their success. As MLs learn English or another language, they go through different phases of language development. They will start in the pre-production phase, where they are mostly silent, communicating with gestures, actions, or a few words. After this phase is the early production where students can say "I don't understand". Then, during speech emergence, students are able to form complete sentences. The last phase is intermediate fluency, being able to produce narratives, write answers, and resolve conflicts (Herrell & Jordan, 2020, p. 20). First, work with your school's world language department to create support and explore different strategies that will work with your students. In an Edutopia article by Michele Lockhart, she writes about students identifying key phrases within their CTE program and compiling a list that will be developed into an individual CTE dictionary (Michele, 2025).

Providing structured routines allows students to reduce anxiety and better focus on learning. Contextualize your directions and be consistent, for example, telling students to grab a textbook and open up to a page. As the teacher, you can grab a textbook and write the page you want students to go to on the board. Be sure to build relationships with your ML students. Use technology to help you. You can use Google Translate or AI to create documents in the students language. Be careful about relying on it as it might not be 100% accurate and could lead to the student being dependent on a translator.

## Other Barriers to Learning

While students may not have an IEP or 504 plan, students may have difficult home lives that impact their learning. Students can be facing ACE; these are external barriers that impact a student's ability to learn. This includes socio-economic barriers like inadequate food, no internet access at home, limited access to health care, or even housing instability. Students may be in foster care, facing homelessness, have parents with mental health issues, exposed to domestic violence, or have parents incarcerated. According to the Center for Disease Control, three in four high school students have reported experiencing one or more ACEs (About Adverse Childhood Experiences | Adverse Childhood Experiences (ACEs), 2024). ACEs can have physical and mental impacts on students. They also may cause students to be the provider for their families, working jobs after school or caring for younger siblings. It is recommended to combat the negative effects of ACEs; students have a positive, supportive relationship with one or more adults (Murphy & Sacks, 2019, p. 10). Further, schools should create programs and opportunities for students to develop key social emotional skills like empathy, self-regulation, and self-efficacy.

How do you support students with these experiences? If a student shares something in confidence that makes you fear for their safety and well-being, it is important you report it right away. You might feel like you are breaking the child's trust, but ensuring student safety is your number one concern. In fact, by reporting, you are providing the necessary intervention that a child often cannot seek for themselves, potentially connecting them to vital resources and protection. It is absolutely critical to know and follow your specific school and district's protocol for reporting suspected child abuse or neglect. This typically involves informing a designated school administrator (e.g., principal, counselor, social worker) who then makes the official report to child protective services. Your school will have clear guidelines on *who* to report to and *what information* to include. If you are informed of a student with ACE, do not ask the student probing questions or bring it up. Keep an eye on the student from a distance. While you may want to do more for a student with ACE, it is important to create a classroom that supports the student. You can:

- Demonstrate Flexibility and Understanding
  By providing grace periods on missed assignments or offering alternative submission methods, you signal to students that their learning is the priority, even when external circumstances interfere with traditional deadlines. This isn't about lowering standards, but about removing unnecessary barriers to demonstrate mastery. Consider a system where students can communicate anticipated difficulties, allowing for proactive adjustments, rather than retroactive penalties.
- Create Safe and Predictable Spaces
  As started in Chapter 1, providing safe and predictable spaces allows students to let their guard down and be part of the classroom. This isn't just about physical safety, but also about creating an emotional environment where students feel respected, understood, and supported. By establishing clear routines, consistent expectations, and a culture of mutual respect, educators can significantly reduce anxiety and uncertainty for all learners. This predictability frees up valuable cognitive resources, allowing students to focus on mastering new skills and building strong connections, rather than expending energy on anticipating the unknown.
- Advocate but Don't Overstep
  While your heart may be to solve every problem a student faces, it's vital to understand and respect professional boundaries. Overstepping your role as an educator can inadvertently create legal or ethical issues, undermine the expertise of other professionals (like counselors or social workers), or even jeopardize a student's privacy or services. Your primary role is to educate, provide a safe classroom, and facilitate connections to appropriate support systems. This is where the school's guidance counselor or social worker becomes your invaluable partner. They are specifically trained and equipped to

navigate the complex landscape of community resources, family services, and legal mandates. They can talk to the students' guidance counselor about providing different support like reaching out to programs that might help students and their families. Some students might need help applying for free and reduced lunch, understanding different county, state, or federal programs available to their families, or identifying their supports.

## Teacher Spotlight

Christian Zimmerman brings a unique perspective to supporting students in post-secondary transition. Currently, at the Florida Center for Students with Unique Abilities located at the University of Central Florida, he assists post-secondary institutions statewide in developing comprehensive transition programs for individuals with intellectual disabilities. His previous experience was the coordinator for How I Reach Employment (HIRE) Program at Lee County Technical Colleges and a prior career in construction, where he focused on disaster restoration. This construction background surprisingly led him to pursue an English degree and teach at a CTE high school, driven by the consistently poor communication skills he observed in job applicants. Zimmerman wanted to help others be successful regardless of their career field. Working in a CTE high school as a core academic teacher, he was able to collaborate on activities with CTE teachers. Zimmerman offers advice for CTE teachers working with students with disabilities and educators helping in their post-secondary transition.

- ♦ The biggest misconception that educators make is that students with disabilities can't do the work. Hands-on learning for students with disabilities is the best way all students can learn.
- ♦ Some programs require students to sit for licensure or certification exams. Teachers may worry

some students may not be able to take the exam. Zimmerman recommends reaching out to the licensing or certification company and talk about accommodations they can offer.
- ♦ There are so many external resources for students. If a student needs a resource, extra support for their learning, or something not offered in the current setting, there are many educators, companies, and organizations helping students.

Students may need some academic remediation to help understand the content and master the skills. The biggest takeaway Zimmerman offered was to meet students where they are and provide as much industry experience, while students are still in high school. He sees students with IEPs be more successful at a post-secondary level after receiving CTE instruction during high school.

As for educators, to be successful, collaborate with other teachers. Go into other CTE and academic classrooms. Sometimes, teachers are hesitant to go into another teacher's classroom, but being able to learn from others, see students in various settings, and collaboration makes the student experience stronger. By simply observing, the teacher observing can learn a new strategy or spark a new idea. Some teachers have a mindset that their industry doesn't give accommodations on the job site. Zimmerman challenges teachers with this mindset to consider school is a place to learn, take a risk, and learn from mistakes. Students are preparing and not on the job site yet so teachers need to prepare them by giving the additional time and support so students can master the skills and be successful later on.

By taking the time to really visualize and ask "what does the IEP and accommodations look like in my classroom?" can help in understanding how to best support the student. Use existing supports to avoid reinventing the wheel and ask for help. Zimmerman highlights the growing and positive trend of middle school CTE exposure and programs, believing that earlier opportunities and support significantly contribute to students' future success.

As our world continues to change, the needs of our students will too. By understanding the specific needs and strengths of all our students, we can unlock the capacity for success. While navigating IEPs, 504 plans, students with ADHD, or those who have experienced ACEs, we can effectively support students. Reach out for help when you need to better serve students. Embrace working with other teachers; everyone holds a shared commitment to ensure each student thrives.

 **Recommended Reading**

- *From Behaving to Belonging: The Inclusive Art of Supporting Students Who Challenge Us* by Julie Causton and Kate MacLeod.
- *Reimagining Special Education: Using Inclusion as a Framework to Build Equity and Support All Students* by Jenna Mancini Rufo and Julie Causton.
- *Outsmart Your Brain: Why Learning is Hard and How You Can Make It Easy* by Daniel T. Willingham.

 **Discussion Questions**

- Reflect on your own CTE program: What specific aspects or activities do you believe make it particularly effective for supporting students with diverse learning styles and needs, leading to their success?
- How can you proactively translate the accommodations and goals outlined in an IEP or 504 plan into daily, meaningful practices within your CTE instruction?

- Who are key individuals within your school (e.g., special education teachers, case managers, counselors) you should actively partner with to better understand and support your students with IEPs/504 plans? What's one question you could ask them this week to strengthen that partnership?

## References

About Adverse Childhood Experiences | Adverse Childhood Experiences (ACEs). (2024, October 8). CDC. Retrieved July 31, 2025. www.cdc.gov/aces/about/index.html

ADHD. (2023, October 5). Understood.org. ADHD. Retrieved July 19, 2025. www.understood.org/en/topics/adhd

Archived: IEP Guide relating to IDEA 97 (does not apply to newer IDEA 2004 Reauthorization) (PDF). (n.d.). Department of Education. Retrieved July 23, 2025. www.ed.gov/sites/ed/files/parents/needs/speced/iepguide/iepguide.pdf

Career and Technical Education: Preparing K–12 Multilingual Learners for Postsecondary Education and Careers. (n.d.). NCELA. Retrieved July 29, 2025. https://ncela.ed.gov/sites/default/files/legacy/files/fast_facts/OELACTEInfographic-20220407-508.pdf

COE – English Learners in Public Schools. (n.d.). National Center for Education Statistics (NCES). Retrieved July 16, 2025. https://nces.ed.gov/programs/coe/indicator/cgf/english-learners-in-public-schools

CRDC Profile of Students with Disabilities in U.S. Public Schools During the 2020-21 School Year. (n.d.). Department of Education. Retrieved July 21, 2025. www.ed.gov/media/document/crdc-student-disabilities-snapshotpdf-21420.pdf

DeLussey, S. (2024). *The Intentional IEP: A Team Approach to Better Outcomes for Students and Their Families*. Wiley.

Dragoo, K. E. (2024, August 20). *The Individuals with Disabilities Education Act (IDEA), Part B: Key Statutory and Regulatory Provisions*. Congress.gov. Retrieved July 31, 2025. www.congress.gov/crs-product/R41833

Herrell, A. L., & Jordan, M. (2020). *50 Strategies for Teaching English Language Learners*. Pearson.

Lee, A. (n.d.). *What is IEP transition planning?* Understood.org. www.understood.org/en/articles/iep-transition-planning-preparing-for-young-adulthood

Michele, L. (2025, July 18). *Combining Career and Technical Education With World Language Instruction*. Edutopia. www.edutopia.org/article/world-languages-career-technical-education/

Morin, A., & Osewalt, G. (2024, March 29). *Classroom Accommodations for ADHD*. Understood.org. Retrieved July 22, 2025. www.understood.org/en/articles/classroom-accommodations-for-adhd

Murphy, D., & Sacks, V. (2019, Summer). Supporting students with adverse childhood experiences. *American Educator*, 43(2), 8–11.

Perkins Briefs: English Learners. (n.d.). Advance CTE. Retrieved July 31, 2025. https://careertech.org/wp-content/uploads/2024/02/Supporting_English_Learners_CTE.pdf

Specific Learning Disabilities. (n.d.). National Center for Learning Disabilities. Retrieved July 19, 2025. https://ncld.org/understand-the-issues/specific-learning-disabilities/

Theobald, R., Plasman, J., Gottfried, M., Gratz, T., Holden, K., & Goldhaber, D. (2022, January/February). Sometimes less, sometimes more: Trends in career and technical education participation for students with disabilities. *Educational Researcher*, 51(1), 40–50. https://doi.org/10.3102/0013189X211006361

Twachtman-Cullen, D., & Twachtman-Bassett, J. (2011). *The IEP from A to Z: How to Create Meaningful and Measurable Goals and Objectives*. Wiley.

Vierstra, G., & Garcia, K. (2024, May 31). *What Is a 504 Plan?* Understood.org. Retrieved July 31, 2025. www.understood.org/en/articles/what-is-a-504-plan

# 8

# The Power of Reflection

Chef Miguel Alfonso stood in my classroom asking for strategies to foster discussion in the classroom. He told me that he wanted to engage his students in discussion, which would lead to writing skills. He even went as far as to observe the English classrooms to better his practice. What I didn't mention to Chef that day was how much I admired his vulnerability and humility to ask for help and try something new in his classroom. Chef is a force in the kitchen, having worked all around the world in numerous restaurants.

Chef was born and raised in the Philippines and wasn't sure what he wanted to pursue. After taking the advice of his sister and father, he went to college in the Philippines for interdisciplinary studies. He fell in love with his classes because they taught him about the world and how to think. Before his junior year, he thought about becoming a chef, and he started working in a restaurant as an apprentice for free. He fell in love with the kitchen and went on to work in a program where he was in a 3-star Michelin restaurant in Spain. Chef will say this experience humbled him, teaching him how important hard work and discipline are. After Spain, his family opened up a fast food restaurant in the Philippines. The difference in working in two opposite restaurants forced him to change his mindset. He thought what can I learn from this experience that I couldn't in a

Michelin star restaurant. His journey eventually led him to come to the United States to attend the Culinary Institute of America. Chef's pathway led him to work in restaurants in Napa Valley, California; Montreal, Canada; and New York City.

Chef eventually left the industry temporarily to raise his children. The hours of a restaurant are hard for a family. His passion for the kitchen never ceased to exist, and his wife suggested becoming a CTE teacher. During his time in New York City, he started a program for restaurant workers to learn English. He knew these language skills were going to help the workers move up in the industry.

When Chef shared his story with me, we initially started talking about his grading practices. He knew from his time in the industry that every single day was a test. Did you show up on time? Did you prep your station? Do you look professional? Did you cut the vegetables correctly? Is the food plated well? He wanted his classroom to reflect this, but struggled to mirror this and provide quality feedback to students. He tried writing down everything that all the students were doing throughout class. This method led him to think about what each restaurant he worked at had in common. What was the common theme to make someone successful in the culinary world? He found the common theme was attitude. In hearing his story, I realized he had the best attitude at every stage of his career. In the moments of hardship, he probably didn't feel like he had the best attitude, but the power to keep going, learning, and giving back is what led him to be confident and ask for help. He eventually developed a rubric to better help his grading practices and provide strong feedback to his students, while allowing him to spend more time helping his students. Chef also started focusing on really honing in on the fundamentals of culinary arts. Like sports, learning the foundations will set star athletes apart from others. Students don't need to constantly be making new dishes, but focus on how they can hone in on one technique every single time.

Throughout Chef Alfonso's incredible journey, a clear theme emerges: his unwavering belief that every experience, no matter how different, holds a valuable lesson. From the demanding pressure of a Michelin-starred kitchen to the fast-paced efficiency of a family restaurant, he continually sought out opportunities to learn and grow. His humility, curiosity, and commitment to lifelong learning were the true "ingredients" of his success. By applying this same mindset to his teaching, he not only transformed his own grading practices and classroom instruction but also modeled for his students the most critical lesson of all: that a positive attitude and a passion for learning are the most powerful tools anyone can have, both in the kitchen and in life.

Our brains never outgrow the desire to learn, and our brains remain malleable (Medina, 2008, p. 252). As educators, we are always striving to do better and learn new strategies to stay current in our field. So, after reading this book, finishing the school year, or just getting through the week, what is next? You'll receive so much advice throughout your first few years teaching, and it never really stops. Some advice will be good and some advice will be bad. I've learned that just because one strategy or idea didn't work for a teacher down the hall, it doesn't mean it won't work for me. To navigate the advice, new students, new program, new school, and everything new, you have to remain true to yourself and your teaching values. Admittedly, I didn't realize the depth of being a CTE teacher until it was the middle of my first year. Being a CTE teacher is the best job I've ever had. I was also surrounded by really strong CTE teachers who excelled at their job. I was curious what common traits CTE teachers had with each other to make them great. These five frames of thinking help CTE teachers remain true to themselves and continue to grow each day:

1. Understand Your Why
2. Be Flexible, Open, and Adaptable
3. Have a Good Attitude
4. Industry Expert and Lifelong Learner
5. Be Student Focused

## Understand Your Why

Think about your why. Why did you go into teaching? Ground yourself in your why before moving forward. Consider what inspires you. In Simon Sinek's book *Start With Why*, energy is good to motivate someone, but charisma inspires (Sinek, 2011, p. 134). Charisma is a clarity of why for someone who inspires one to do more and continue to show up each day (Sinek, 2011, p. 135). Define your own why and your core inspiration that will fuel you for each day. Being able to anchor yourself in your core beliefs helps to bring passion and energy that is infectious to those around you. More importantly, defining your why isn't just an exercise; it is the foundation of each thing you do. On the hard days of teaching, knowing your why is critical. It keeps you going, it renews your hope, and it serves as a foundation.

## Be Flexible, Open, and Adaptable

"That won't work in my classroom". I've heard countless statements that are negative about a new strategy, initiative, or problem that arises. It is easy to be negative and a default when change is threatening us. Sometimes, we don't always get to see the why of a decision, and most of the time, we have no control when it comes to student behavior, angry parents, or changes in the school district. While you may know 100% that something won't work, try it anyway. You might learn something new about yourself, students, or coworkers.

As the saying goes, sh-- happens. Power goes out at school, students break lab equipment, and much more will happen. Being able to roll with it and adapt will not only help you, but it will keep you sane. You can't control everything that happens as much as you might plan for something. Unfortunately, bigger disruptions happen too. Your school administration can affect your project because of state mandates or severe budget cuts. You can get a new supervisor or superintendent that has a different vision.

## Have a Good Attitude

Similar to being flexible, your attitude is contagious to students and your colleagues. Each day you have students that could be dealing with their own issues at home but come to your classroom wanting to learn. Avoid complaining about your boss, the topic you are covering in class, or other students. Mayo Clinic shares the benefits of positive thinking: increased life span, lower rates of depression, greater resistance to illness, and better coping skills during hardships (Positive Thinking: Reduce Stress by Eliminating Negative Self-Talk, n.d.). If you find yourself to be a person that looks at the glass half empty instead, surround yourself with positive people, be open to humor, and practice positive talk. Some easy ways to do this are by saying "let's take a chance", "I can try and make it work", or "it's an opportunity to learn something new" (Positive Thinking: Reduce Stress by Eliminating Negative Self-Talk, n.d.). This attitude is infectious and makes each day a little bit easier. Try one small change!

## Industry Expert and Lifelong Learner

I would never try to explain how to change a tire or oil to my coworkers that teach automotive technology. But, I might offer different instructional strategies to them to try in their classrooms. You are the industry expert that holds all the content knowledge. The hardest part of CTE is blending that content knowledge with instructional strategies. Own your knowledge but also continue learning. Having a growth mindset that empowers you to keep growing as a learner is a powerful driver. You and your students reap the benefits. Consider continuing your education as an industry expert. Your school might pay for you to take classes or attend professional development.

My colleagues were feverishly jotting down notes as my student, Evan, was talking about ways to use AI in the classroom. Evan had spent weeks conducting research, surveying students, and using AI tools to design a professional development for teachers. When I first started a professional development series for staff members at my school led by my students, some of my colleagues were eager to support but didn't expect to learn so much for my students. Teachers were pleasantly surprised by how informative and meaningful the strategies Evan offered. They also appreciated the extensive research he did. Don't count someone out just because of their age, academic degree, or perceived skill level.

**Professional Learning**: My colleagues and I slowly walked into the cafeteria where we had a 3-hour professional development session. The professional development speaker was waiting for us with a smile. Everyone had already grumbled about having a speaker and listed off the other things they could be doing instead. As the speaker started her presentation, she won everyone over quickly. Her strategies and presentation were bite sized, meaning every single strategy she presented, we could use tomorrow if we wanted. She also told us funny stories about her failures which made her relatable. Everyone was pleasantly surprised and started to be more open about making some changes.

There are many unique struggles as a CTE teacher. Many CTE teachers find themselves as the sole instructor for their specific program within a school building. Being able to discuss lesson plans, curriculum, and industry with another person teaching the same program is extremely valuable. Constantly staying up to date with the industry while balancing the demanding classroom can be a challenge. Each year, you are going to be required to attend professional development. A constant complaint I hear from CTE teachers is the lack of personalized professional development. Sometimes, school will have a focus for the school year and bring in speakers that don't always fully understand what CTE teachers do. Some speakers will be better than others. I urge you to give them a chance. Even one strategy can be useful in transforming your practice even if that person teaches a different subject from you.

However, advocate for meaningful and personalized professional development. Give feedback to administration on the professional learning days they plan each year. Ask questions regarding finding your own professional learning. Suggest a speaker. Ask to attend a workshop related to your industry. I like to believe that schools have their staff and students' best interest in mind, but sometimes there is mixed messaging and things get lost in translation. Another strategy is asking about externships. Contacting other CTE teachers that teach similar programs and asking to shadow can open up new possibilities, form strong relationships, and improve practice.

One of my guilty habits is watching TV to relax. I found myself watching the *Great British Baking Show* on Netflix one weekend. Participants go through three different rounds of baking: a signature bake showing their creative flair, a technical bake where one basic recipe is used, and a showstopper bake (About the Show, n.d.). Each round is harder than the last. Toward the end of the fourth episode I watched, I reflected. Why can't I implement a similar model in my classroom? On the first day of instruction, students engage in a signature activity. Students engage in an activity that practices foundational skills they have learned, much like a baker's creative take on a well-known recipe. This allows them to demonstrate their initial understanding and personal flair. On the second day of instruction, students reflect and learn new skills or concepts. Day 3 is a technical activity. Students are given a challenge or prompt that requires them to apply the new skills they just learned. This is a formative assessment – a chance to see if they can execute the skills independently and receive targeted feedback without the pressure of a final project. Then, day 4 and day 5 are a showstopper – students use all the skills and feedback they developed to produce something on their own. While I don't teach culinary, the model was extremely beneficial to my students. The best professional learning often happens when you have an "aha moment". Inspiration can spark from anywhere and anyone. Like our students, we need room to try something, make a mistake, and reevaluate. Find a group of educators that teach a similar program and partner with them. Sharing ideas, creating projects, and venting about issues can help a teacher feel connected, excited, and hopeful.

**Join Organizations**: The dynamic nature of industry and teaching practices makes staying current a continuous effort. Joining professional organizations that provide shared resources, research insights, and strategic approaches is a valuable way to remain informed. Financial support from your school district might even be available for individual and student memberships. These often include access to monthly journals, newsletters, website content, and networking events. Given the multitude of organizations with similar aims, prioritizing those that genuinely inspire and align with your professional values is essential for meaningful engagement. Some professions require license recertifications to maintain active status. Ask your school if you are able to use professional development time to recertify, take classes, and expand your expertise. By remaining active in the industry, it restores energy and renews ideas.

Once you are part of different organizations, think about collaborating with them for your students. They might be willing to sponsor students in the workplace, donate materials or resources, and serve as guest speakers. Remaining active in the organization can also reenergize your own passion and connection to the industry.

**Engage in Fellowships**: For educators seeking to deepen their expertise and broaden their influence, a fellowship can be a transformative experience. These are short-term opportunities that empower teachers to engage in meaningful work related to a specific topic, often with a stipend. They are a powerful pathway for teacher leadership, providing a platform and the tools to grow your influence beyond the four walls of your classroom. CTE teachers are unique teachers that other educators can learn from. Fellowships often have a specific purpose and theme. The landscape can be diverse:

- Advocacy and Policy: Fellowships like 50CAN is a national program that gives fellows tools to advocate for better education. Fellows will learn from leaders in the education reform space to draft Op-eds, speaking events, social media posts, or news articles to advocate for their chosen educational issue. It provides a platform and tools to help grow the teacher leader.
- Subject–Matter Expertise: Other fellowships are designed to advance a subject. For instance, the National Science Foundation offers fellowships for science and math teachers to engage in cutting-edge research. This also can extend to CTE teachers. The Association for Career and Technical Education also offers a fellowship for CTE teachers.

- Curriculum and Research: Many fellowships are project-based, requiring fellows to research, design, or pilot new curriculum. These experiences often culminate in a presentation, published paper, or creation of a new course.

Typically, the terms are determined by the organization and include some type of task completion by the end of the fellowship. This deliverable can look like research, producing curriculum, presenting at a conference, or engaging in advocacy work. Some fellowships will require you to have permission from your school district. If you are considering a fellowship, think about these questions before applying:

- What are the core values of the fellowship?
- What type of time commitment is the fellowship?
- What specific skills will I learn?
- How does this fellowship align with my future goals?
- What are some potential challenges?

By choosing a fellowship that genuinely resonates with your professional identity, you invest in a path of continuous learning that will not only advance your own career but provide your students with a more knowledgeable, connected, and inspired teacher.

## Be Student Focused

The argument is made each year that the students have changed. Yes, they have. Students are exposed to technology, media, and changes at a younger age. They live in a fast-paced world where there are constant ups and downs. They are starting to demand better from us as educators. We need to accept that and reimagine what school should be for these students. As you think of your classroom, projects, and opportunities, be student focused. How are students at the core of instruction and each decision you make? Consider if there are better ways of teaching something than how you learned. Involve the students in making decisions, give them choices, and hold them accountable.

## Reflection

"I should have done this differently." These words live in my head a lot during the school year. During your first years of teaching, it may seem that reflection is out of reach. With the demands of a new job, it can be hard to find time to truly reflect. Reflection and growth are necessary steps for educators and students. Reflection and growth don't have to happen at marked times like the end of the school year. Many CTE teachers enter education as a second career. You have a wealth of industry experience and are an expert in the field. Learning a new career while fusing a profession can be challenging. Teaching is a complex sport. The constant mindset to continue growing, evolving, and transforming will allow a program to find growth.

You can find ways to engage in regular personal reflection. There are different apps you can download on your phone to remind you to pause for reflection. Establishing a dedicated time to reflect is helpful but not always realistic. Capturing your thoughts when they arise or during your dedicated reflection time helps capture your ideas and make notes. I like being able to write something down and go back to it later. Similarly, some teachers like to use voice notes or memos to record their thoughts and reflect.

There will be pointed times that you will be forced to reflect or engage in group reflection. After each teacher evaluation, you will reflect on the lesson and discuss it with the evaluator. While the evaluation process is meant to help teachers, the reflection process might seem surface level. I encourage you to really use this opportunity to reflect on your lesson.

Professional Learning Communities (PLC) are groups of teachers that typically teach the same subject or grade level. As a CTE teacher, we are often the only instructor of the subject in our school. Having a PLC with other CTE instructors in the school can still be beneficial because of the shared structure and challenges. PLCs typically meet on a regular basis to discuss ways to improve learning and student achievement. They build strong relationships between members, help teachers stay on top of new research and tools, and help reflect on ideas (Serviss, n.d.).

Similar to PLCs, Critical Friends Group (CFG) offers a model for reflection and support. This is a group of peers committed to meeting regularly to improve their practice. The National School Reform Faculty created this model so teachers can use protocols to use cycles of action-research to achieve better results (National School Reform Faculty, 2025). The group supports one another in improving practices. Ultimately, both PLCs and CFGs combat the professional isolation many teachers feel. They transform the educational environment from a collection of individual classrooms into a collaborative hub where teachers collectively grow, improve their craft, and, most importantly, work together to achieve better outcomes for their students.

During my first few years teaching, I had a supervisor that was relentless. It felt like no matter what I did, I was doing it wrong. Each week she should come into my classroom for a walk through or "pop-in". She would silently walk in, walk around the room or sit at a desk, and listen for 10 to 15 minutes. After, she would carefully leave. Within the half hour, I had a calendar invite to discuss the pop-in. I would complain to my colleagues each time this happened which happened once a week! My colleagues didn't receive these pop-ins as frequently as I did or calendar invites for feedback. I felt like I was the only one doing a bad job. Looking back, I can say that it made me work harder and focus on classroom management that I probably wouldn't have focused on without the push of my supervisor. I was so laser focused on teaching the content that I wasn't strategic about classroom management or even thought about it. I also can see her intentions were good and she wanted to support me.

Teacher evaluations happen each year, typically multiple times. Each school adopts their own evaluation model. Some schools choose to use a nationally recognized model like The Framework for Teaching Model by the Danielsol Group or The Marzano Focused Teacher Evaluation Model. Other schools might develop their own system for evaluations. Classroom instruction, classroom culture, professionalism, and planning for instruction are common categories in the evaluation model. Common categories across these models include classroom instruction, classroom culture, professionalism, and planning for instruction. Each model offers a rubric to guide teacher practice, giving educators a shared language for what excellence looks like.

It's helpful to view an observation not as a final judgment, but as a snapshot of the overall picture of your teaching. To ensure that your evaluator sees the full scope of your work beyond that single moment, consider proactively providing evidence of your teaching practice. This might include sharing a lesson plan with a clear alignment to learning standards, showcasing a collection of student work from a project, or presenting data from a formative assessment.

If your observation is announced, use this to your advantage. Rather than simply asking the observer what they want to see, frame the conversation around your own professional growth. For example, you might say, "I've been working on improving my use of questioning to promote critical thinking. I'd appreciate it if you could specifically focus on that during the observation and provide feedback". This not only demonstrates your commitment to continuous improvement but also guides the observer to give you targeted, useful feedback. Ultimately, the evaluation process is a tool for professional development, and by approaching it with a strategic and reflective mindset, you can turn a routine requirement into a meaningful opportunity to refine your craft.

### Reflection and Students

Students often forget to stop and reflect on their learning, growth, and time. Building in purposeful reflection allows students to find deeper learning, make stronger connections, and develop greater self-awareness of their strengths, challenges, and progress. Exit tickets often fall to the wayside because of time. Marking periods, mid marking periods, and the end of the school year are good places to stop and reflect with students. Learning to be more reflective creates a more integrated brain, when teens learn to relate to one other and have reflective conversations.

Students can teach us a lot when given the right tools and platform. That doesn't mean students are in control. Having various protocols and routines to reflect and review performance.

A SWOT analysis is a strategy to help identify **Strengths**, **Weaknesses**, **Opportunities**, and **Threats** (What Is SWOT? – SWOT Analysis – Research Guides at Baruch College, n.d.). As a result of completing a SWOT analysis, it helps you plan in the future.

- What strengths do I have as a teacher?
- What weaknesses does my program have?
- What opportunities can I take advantage of?
- What threats are harming my program?

Other ways to use a SWOT analysis:

- Students can engage in a SWOT analysis for career planning, on major projects, and industry scenarios.
- The advisory council can use this strategy to identify different areas to enhance the program.

## Teacher Well-Being

I found myself drowning in work at school, and most of it wasn't even related to the classroom. I had become a class advisor, club advisor to two different clubs, served on two different committees, planning my school's CTE Month celebration and Bring Your Child to Work Day. I wanted to be so involved that I lost sight of what brought me joy and my why. There was an expectation to do well at all of it while also teaching my students. I lost sight of what the whole purpose was and what fueled me each day. I even thought about taking a day off work to try and catch up on grading, lesson planning, and all the other tasks I had to complete.

Self-care isn't selfish. Saying no is okay. These two sentences are something I heard many times but yet, the moment I needed to say no or wanted to do something for myself, the guilt sank in my stomach. I had a hard time saying no. Why can we give advice to others and hear the warnings but fail to listen to ourselves? As educators, we are smart humans. We all know how important it is to sleep well, stay hydrated, eat well, and exercise, but we often ignore it. Why? We always feel the urge that we have to accomplish the next thing or something will fail without us. I am guilty of it too. I always dread when I call out at the last minute due to a family emergency or being sick because I know it puts a strain on the staff to cover my classes and I worry about the students. In reality, the day went on without me. The school building didn't go up in flames because I wasn't there. Being uncomfortable in those moments can help for the future. Teaching requires us to be on constantly and interact with students who need a lot from us. Taking moments for ourselves to recharge and refresh is important.

Making a change is hard. I find myself saying next marking period I will reintroduce our class rules and I'll change how ... I like fresh starts and pointed places in time. In Mike Anderson's book Rekindle Your Professional Fire, he cites Katy Milkman's fresh start effect (Anderson, 2024, p. 113). He urges educators to jump right into change, pick a good time to change. Look at natural ways that you can start a change. The first year of teaching will seem like a whirlwind. But it is also full of excitement, learning, and laughs. As you embark on your journey as a CTE teacher, remember that you stand at the pivotal intersection of education and industry, uniquely positioned to shape not just careers, but lives. Embrace the continuous learning, lean into collaboration, and always remember the profound impact you have. Your dedication to fostering real-world skills and igniting individual potential makes you an indispensable force in preparing the workforce of tomorrow.

Unfortunately, teacher burnout is a serious problem that continues to plague the education system. It stems from chronic, unmanaged stress often brought on by heavy workloads, challenging student behaviors, insufficient resources, lack of administrative support, and feelings of being underappreciated or undervalued. This state of exhaustion not only negatively impacts a teacher's well-being, leading to increased stress, anxiety, and even physical health problems, but also significantly affects the quality of instruction, student engagement, and, ultimately, student outcomes. In a recent survey, it cited managing student behavior as the top source of stress followed by salary being too low and administrative work outside of teaching (Walker, 2025). These challenges are systematic and not easily fixable. So, how does one navigate the challenges of becoming a new CTE teacher and avoiding burnout? The first step is taking care of your own needs first. Drinking water, getting enough sleep, and being aware of how you are feeling are most important. Next, finding a positive support system is key. Use tools from this book and the people around you to take care of yourself. Listen to a podcast, watch a show, or schedule time for rest on the weekend. Reaching out for help and being open to changes can help avoid burnout.

## Celebrate Others and Yourself

Teaching is a deeply rewarding profession, and for most educators, the greatest fulfillment comes from seeing their students grow and achieve success. On the other hand, acknowledging the hard work and passion of teachers is a vital component of a healthy educational ecosystem. Celebrating one another, whether for small wins or significant accomplishments, builds a positive culture of support and professional validation.

Beyond the intrinsic rewards, external recognition from organizations, companies, and local businesses serves as a powerful testament to a teacher's impact. When looking at the different awards available, consider the qualifications carefully. Awards can vary widely, focusing on a specific content area (e.g., a science, technology, engineering, and mathematics (STEM) educator award), a particular number of years in the field, or excellence in a specific practice like innovation or community engagement.

Don't be afraid to apply for local, state, or even national teaching awards. The process itself is a valuable exercise in self-reflection and professional documentation. When considering an application, think about what makes your practice unique. Have you developed an innovative project, achieved a significant outcome with students, or built a powerful community partnership? Documenting these successes throughout the year makes the application process much easier. Additionally, actively nominate a deserving colleague. The act of championing someone else's work is not only rewarding but also contributes to a culture where excellence is celebrated and shared.

## Teacher Spotlight

I was sharing ways to make your classroom more real-world at a conference when a woman raised her hand and said this is great but … I was excited by her interruption. She wanted to know more about designing a model where students were working with real clients. In talking with her, she shared she was an automotive technology teacher in Jamaica. Tracy-Ann Hall is not just a teacher, but a mentor, advocate, and national role model. Her story and determination really impacted my own thoughts about what makes a great teacher.

Her love of teaching and mentoring started when she was working in a local garage teaching trainees how to repair cars. Her motivation for overcoming failure is an inspiration. She was initially denied from the Vocational Training Development Institute (VTDI) because she lacked the qualifications. Instead of giving up on her dream, she earned a diploma in Supervisory Management and then was accepted in the VTDI. She wanted to be a role model for teens as she struggled with learning from a young age. She was diagnosed with dyslexia and was told by many she would fail school. A principal even told her was retarded for not being able to sit still and wanting to use her hands for playing. This attitude stayed with her in high school where she failed most of her subjects. Through her own personal hardships, like her mom being diagnosed with breast cancer, being rejected by the VTDI, and having to move home to take care of her mom, her attitude has remained the same. She wants to show that the undervalued person has meaning and purpose.

She said most of her students are considered students who are failures. Her outlook on them is completely different. Her focus is on creating students ready to take on the world. She knows each student is more than capable of being successful given the right tools. Tracy-Ann ensures her students don't take no for an answer and believes in themselves. Hall believes classrooms should feel like workshops—dynamic, hands-on, and full of possibility. She involves parents in the learning process and makes a concerted effort to support students with learning challenges, much like the ones she faced. She integrates charts of student achievements and goal setting walls, uses friendly competitions, and rewards effort and progress. She has also secured scholarships for exceptional students by partnering with leaders in the automotive industry. Hall even set up a classroom library, encouraging book reviews and fostering a culture of learning. Her students were the first group in the school's history to achieve a 95% pass rate on their testing.

Her classroom needed to be repainted, but she was told there was no money to repaint the classroom. With the combined efforts of herself and her students, she was able to get donations for paint and supplies. The community came together to repaint her classroom, including motivational and safety signs. She launched other community initiatives like feeding the homeless, starting a junior automotive club, and joining school committees. With resources scarce, she has been ingenious in finding materials and components for her automotive classes, which are difficult to attract funding for, again forming partnerships with those in the automotive sector to use their facilities and spare parts.

In 2017, she was selected among ten finalists from 20,000 global applicants for the Varkey Foundation Global Teacher Prize. She planned to use the prize to upgrade her automotive lab at Jonathan Grant High School to international standards. Her goals included securing diagnostic machines, wheel-balancing tools, and other vital training equipment. Unfortunately, Hall didn't win but was able to network and learn from teachers around the world. Since 2017, she

> has been named the Technical and Vocational Education and Training (TVET) Teacher of the Year at the Ministry of Education, Skills, Youth and Information Awards. She emphasized the importance of technical skills for students from disadvantaged backgrounds, many of whom must work before pursuing higher education. She was also appointed master teacher by the Jamaican Teaching Council.
> 
> To date, she has trained over 1,000 automotive students. She is committed to continue to educate, train, inspire, and elevate the next generation of automotive technicians in Jamaica and around the world. Her story serves as inspiration to never give up and keep students centered.

So, what's next? Education can be a lifelong learning journey. Each year, you may have the same curriculum, but you have different students and can teach it an infinite amount of ways. Accomplishing your first marking period, first year, and first five years of teaching are accomplishments. If you find yourself losing sight of the purpose or you aren't achieving enough, reflect on this "achievement comes when you pursue and attain what you want. Success comes when you are in clear pursuit of why you want it" (Sinek, 2011, p. 181). The quote is a powerful reminder that if you're feeling lost or unmotivated, you shouldn't just chase new achievements. Instead, you should reflect on your "why" – the purpose that gives your work a deeper sense of meaning and ultimately leads to success. You might fail on your journey; failure can be good, but it doesn't always feel like it in the moment. Give yourself grace and start again tomorrow.

 **Recommended Reading**

- *Hidden Potential* by Adam Grant.
- *Start With Why* by Simon Sinek.
- *Reset* by Dan Heath.

 **Discussion Questions**

- What are your core aspirations or key areas of focus for the current school year, both for your students' learning and for your own professional growth?
- How will you intentionally and purposefully build moments for meaningful reflection into your busy teaching schedule this year?
- What is one non-negotiable self-care practice you will commit to protecting to ensure your sustained impact and joy in teaching?

## Beginning of the Year Checklist

The start of the school year always feels like a whirlwind. This checklist encompasses many things you will need to think about as a first year teacher. Some of the items are annual tasks that need to be done.

**First Year Checklist**

- Know the main parts of the building.
  - Nurses Office, School Counselor Office, Main Office, Security, and Staff Lounge/Copy Room.
  - Know your fire exits.
- Ask for a tutorial about all learning management systems.
  - Grading Platform
    - How to enter grades, weigh assignments?
    - What grading categories do I need to have?
    - How often do I need to enter grades?
  - Lesson Plans
    - Do I need to submit them? Format? How often do we submit them?

- Teacher Evaluation Platform
    - Where can I see my scores and feedback?
    - What evidence do I need to upload?
- Absences
    - How many absences am I allowed? What types of absences?
    - What rules are in place? For example, you must submit for a personal day 5 days in advance or you can't take off before a long weekend or break.
- Purchase Orders
    - Create a system for tracking purchase orders and invoices (this will come in handy as you have a budget you need to work with).
- Payroll
    - How can I see my paystubs?
    - Do I need to submit timesheets for extracurricular activities?
- Understand your assigned duties on campus.
    - Do you have to attend lunch duty? After school extra help?
- Find out about end of course testing and what credentials you want to offer students.

**Annual Checklist**

- Complete any online training modules required.
- Enter the classroom and prioritize what needs to be set up for the first few days.
- Test all equipment in your lab and find out what works and what does not.
    - Technology
        - Do you have a laptop and/or desktop? How do you print and make copies?
        - Does your SmartBoard work?
    - Tools, Materials, and Machines

- Have a vision of what you would like the classroom/lab to look like for the first marking period. Account for safety parameters in the classroom.
    - Use students to accomplish your vision – do not attempt to do this alone.
- Print out roster for fire drills, etc./prepare your emergency folder.
- Establish your expectations from students.
    - What rules and procedures are non-negotiable?
- Understand what IEPs and 504 plans are and see how these relate to your classroom.

## References

About the Show. (n.d.). The Great British Bake Off. Retrieved August 1, 2025. https://thegreatbritishbakeoff.co.uk/about-the-show/

Anderson, M. (2024). *Rekindle Your Professional Fire: Powerful Habits for Becoming a More Well-Balanced Teacher*. ASCD.

National School Reform Faculty. (2025). *Bring CFG® Work to Your School or Organization!* National School Reform Faculty. https://nsrfharmony.org/whatiscfgwork/

Positive Thinking: Reduce Stress by Eliminating Negative Self-Talk. (n.d.). Mayo Clinic. Retrieved July 21, 2025. www.mayoclinic.org/healthy-lifestyle/stress-management/in-depth/positive-thinking/art-20043950

Serviss, J. (n.d.). 4 Benefits of an Active Professional Learning Community | ISTE. ISTE. Retrieved July 31, 2025. https://iste.org/blog/4-benefits-of-an-active-professional-learning-community

Sinek, S. (2011). *Start with Why: How Great Leaders Inspire Everyone to Take Action*. Penguin.

Walker, T. (2025, April 7). *What's Causing Teacher Burnout? | NEA*. National Education Association. Retrieved July 22, 2025. www.nea.org/nea-today/all-news-articles/whats-causing-teacher-burnout

What Is SWOT? – SWOT Analysis – Research Guides at Baruch College. (n.d.). Research Guides. Retrieved July 18, 2025. https://guides.newman.baruch.cuny.edu/swot

For Product Safety Concerns and Information please contact our EU
representative GPSR@taylorandfrancis.com
Taylor & Francis Verlag GmbH, Kaufingerstraße 24, 80331 München, Germany

www.ingramcontent.com/pod-product-compliance
Lightning Source LLC
Chambersburg PA
CBHW061440300426
44114CB00014B/1773